# NO BULLIES

# NO BULLIES

## **Solutions** for Saving Our Children from **Today's** Bully

Bobby Kipper
and Bud Ramey

New York

**NO BULLIES**
**Solutions** for Saving Our Children from **Today's** Bully



Published in New York, New York, by Morgan James Publishing. Morgan James and The Entrepreneurial Publisher are trademarks of Morgan James, LLC.
www.MorganJamesPublishing.com



ISBN 978-1-61448-437-0 paperback
ISBN 978-1-61448-438-7 eBook
Library of Congress Control Number: 2012950936

**Cover Design by:**
Chris Treccani
www.3dogdesign.net

**Interior Design by:**
Bonnie Bushman
bonnie@caboodlegraphics.com

# Contents


Foreword ix

A Global Crisis – 25 Countries xii

It's Not *If*, It's *When* Your Child Will Be Bullied.
And Here's What Your Child Shouldn't Do xiii

**"Just Tell Me What to Do..." xx**

**The Culture of Bullying — What Is It Really About and Why Are So Many Young People Embracing It? 1**

Bullying Defined 4

How Bullying Got Out of Control 5

Let's Dispel the Myths About Bullying 10

Understand All Five Traditional Forms of Bullying 13

At What Age Does Bullying Become a Danger to Kids? 15

Between Meanness and Bullying 17

What Bullying and Gangs Have in Common 19

**"Just Tell Me What To Do..." 21**

**Preparing Our Children For Bullying Encounters 23**

Leave Nothing Unsaid with Your Child:
Have Regular "Bully Talks" 25

Making the Distinction Between Self-Esteem and Selfish Esteem 28

The Potential Impact of Bullying 30

Ten Suggestions To Help Your Child Navigate Around the Bullies 31

The Bully. The Victim. The Bystander.
Why Bystanders Have the Power 33

Rehearse for the Show: Use Role Play to
Practice Reactions to Bullying 37

Kids May Not Love Every Classmate, But They Understand Politeness 41
Differences and Diversity Are Wonderful, but Avoid Social Isolation 44
Personality Will Impact How Your Child Responds to a Bullying Situation 48
Brothers and Sisters Will Have Conflict, Constantly; Minimize the Chaos By Not Buying Into the Provoking Behaviors 50
Carefully Observe Your Child's Friends 52

**Early Warnings 53**
Be Skeptical of Teasing 55
Watch for Warning Signs of Today's Bully 58
Is Your Child Becoming a Bully? Be Alert to These Indicators 60

**Your Reaction To Bullying 63**
Important Do's and Don'ts 65
It Is a Crime To Assault Another Person; It Is Also a Civil Case 67
The Four Things You Should Never Do 68
Kids Can Be Slow to Reveal Being Bullied: Signs to Watch for 69
The Five Kinds of Bullies Today 71
Be Alert for Signs of Self-Harm Risk in a Bullied Child 73

**Social Media Threats 79**
New Digital Dangers That May Be Invisible to Parents 81
You Are Paying the Bill: Control Your Child's Social Media 86
When Cyberbullying Becomes a Crime 91

**The Bullying Child 93**
Physical Bullying is a Boys' World 95
Girl Bullies Use Different Weapons 99
If Your Child Becomes a Bully, New Ground Rules Are Essential 102

**The Bullied Child 105**
Confronting the Parents 107
Teach Your Child to Stand Firm 109
Twelve Things to Consider When Your Child Has Been Bullied 111

Bullying of Any Kind Can Result in Lifelong Emotional Damage and Why Professional Counseling Should Be Considered 114
Do Children Grow Out of Bullying? 117
Get Involved and Monitor Your Child's School Environment 120
Understand What Your School Should Be Doing When Bullying Occurs 122

**Youth Sports** **129**
Adult Bully Behavior Needs to Be Challenged 131

**Four Promises** **135**
Four Special Promises By You And Your Child 137
Appendix 139
Acknowledgements 153
Endnotes 155
Bibliography 167
No COLORS 171
NCPCV 173
Green Zone™ 176
Virginia Tech's Actively Caring for People 178

# GREEN ZONE

| Behavior | Recommended Intervention |
| --- | --- |
| Using a normal rate, tone, and volume of speech | (None) |
| Complimenting or encouraging others | (None) |
| Informally questioning others | (None) |
| Joking in a non-harmful manner | (None) |

# YELLOW ZONE

| Behavior | Recommended Intervention |
| --- | --- |
| Name-calling and put-downs | Group intervention *and* individual intervention as necessary |
| Intentionally excluding individuals | Group intervention *and* individual intervention as necessary. |
| Damaging another's reputation | Group intervention *and* individual intervention as necessary. |
| Spreading rumors | Group intervention *and* individual intervention as necessary. |
| Manipulating friendships or other relationships | Group intervention *and* individual intervention as necessary. |

# RED ZONE

| Behavior | Recommended Intervention |
| --- | --- |
| Using profane or abusive language | Individual intervention and legal consequences if necessary. |
| Threatening or intimidating others | Individual intervention and legal consequences if necessary. |
| Harassing others based on their race, gender, sexual orientation, personal beliefs, or any other physical or personal characteristic. | |

---

### The Green Zone™

Introducing the Green Zone™, a powerful new, measurable, and affordable anti-bullying and civility campaign for schools and public venues. "Imagine living in a world where everyone treated each other with respect; a world without insults, profanity, or threats, where everyone spoke to each other using a normal rate, tone and volume of speech. If this is the environment you wish to live and be involved with, welcome to the GreenZone™.

# Foreword

### *By Tom Emswiller*

**Bullying gets a lot** of attention these days. Over the past several years the anti-bullying cause has also gathered its share of celebrity advocates. No one should doubt the value of that particular spotlight or the sincerity of those who help direct it. In fact, the intensity and scope of that illumination has helped raise needed awareness and educate a great many people while also supporting the efforts of those on the frontlines of the bullying epidemic.

Most important of all, this growing focus and the information and communications it generates have, in what we hope is a large and growing number of cases, improved the situation for the victims of the bully.

If there's a concern, it's that spotlights sometimes move. Attention has a way of shifting. New and important causes come into being. But the bully and the social and personal devastation he or she creates don't go away. That's why Bud Ramey and Bobby Kipper wrote this book.

***"No BULLIES"*** is much more than a companion piece to Ramey and Kipper's informative and best selling book, "***No COLORS.***" It's an extension of the threat level they raised for some of the highly dangerous behaviors they first examined in their comprehensive look at gangs and youth violence.

While Ramey and Kipper point out some very strong similarities and relationships between gang behavior and bullying, they are also clear about the important differences. For example, all bullies aren't gang members and, conversely, all gang members aren't bullies — though a high percentage may be. Even more telling, as "***No COLORS***" continually emphasizes, gangs exist and thrive in places you can't even imagine or don't want to. But bullies are spread out across the human landscape in even greater numbers. And they exist within every thread of our social fabric.

From classrooms, athletic fields, boardrooms, shop floors and government buildings to movie sets, faculty lounges, seminaries, construction sites and homes somebody is getting bullied. And from the local and national political arena, the news media and the entertainment industry to the cubicle, the bus stop and everywhere in between, somebody is doing the bullying.

That means we've all seen bullies in action. Many of us have been the victims. Some of us have been the perpetrator. Thanks to all the attention being focused on bullies and the issues that surround them, most of us are getting the information we need. But if we're raising children in this culture of bullying or if we're part of the village that helps, we also need some effective and user-friendly tools to go up against the bully. We need some very specific and action-oriented strategies to help every child feel welcomed and valued. And that's the other reason why Ramey and Kipper wrote this book.

What they tell us throughout this very important work is that together, we can build a more civil and less dangerous world for ourselves and those who will follow us. And nobody every built anything worthwhile without the right tools.

**Tom Emswiller**

San Jose, CA

"It doesn't stop at the schoolyard or even a child's front door. Access to the Internet and social media websites mean kids can be bullied and tormented around the clock, even in the supposed safety of their own homes. The cruelty that can come with the strike of a button on a keyboard can hurt just as much as any punch or push in a playground."

**—Anderson Cooper, CNN, February 28, 2013**

# A Global Crisis – 25 Countries

TO UNDERSTAND THE ISSUE of bullying from a global perspective, in 2012, Microsoft commissioned a survey to examine a range of online behaviors among youth – from "meanness" (least severe) to online bullying or cruelty (most severe), and everything in between.

- Fifty-four percent of children age eight to seventeen in twenty-five countries express concern that they will be bullied online.
- Four in ten say someone was mean to them online.
- Nearly one-quarter (24 percent) admits to having bullied someone else online at one time or another.

*Introduction*

# It's Not *If*, It's *When* Your Child *Will* Be Bullied. And Here's *What* Your Child Shouldn't Do

ONE OF THE DIRECTIONS we decided against when we initially planned "***No BULLIES***" was relating other people's experiences about being bullied. It's not that we didn't have a lot of stories. It seems like every one we talked to wants to share his or her tale of bully misery, which almost always occurred sometime from the 6th grade to their senior year in high school. There were earlier and later time periods covered in the many experiences people told us about, but most fell into that classic pre-teen and later adolescent time slot.

The reason we decided not to document those stories or create case studies was because there are quite a few venues already existing for that kind of information. In order to stay true to our promise of providing what you can't find easily if at all from these other sources — practical interventions designed to answer the parental question, "what can I do?" — we fought the urge at times to transform "***No BULLIES***" into a collection of shared experience. That's an important and worthy contribution. But it's not the one we wish to make.

With just this one little exception. It's a true story that played out for one of your authors, Bud Ramey, and we chose to include it not because it's more interesting or valuable than anyone else's, but because it's a cautionary tale.

**"Today, the kind of action I finally took, which gave me an undeniable sense of redemption and made my dad so proud when I finally told him about it, could be a gateway to horror"**

Just about everything your child shouldn't do is contained in this story and it is also a straightforward and clearly understood example of why Today's Bully is not your father's bully, or probably not yours either for that matter. Because this is Bud's story, he's going to tell it in his own words:

> For some reason that will remain forever unknown to me, or perhaps for no reason at all, I was tormented by a football player who loomed over me in height and was probably close to twice my weight. He would slam me into lockers as we walked down the hall, push me against the wall when there were no lockers to offer that distinct metallic clatter and punch me in the arms, the stomach and the back whenever no one in authority was looking. His name was Wayne. I suppose it still is.
>
> It had been going on for months and like many bully encounters, the stomach churning fear bothered me even more than the punches. What stays in my memory is how I would constantly look around to see if he was in the vicinity. And it seemed like he always was.
>
> The lavatories at school. Walking home or sitting on the bus. In the neighborhood, even when I kept changing my normal routes. It didn't matter. He was determined and flexible enough to turn any

of my choices into a continuous back and forth movement along a fear continuum that ranged from mild anxiety to flop sweat.

At times I thought that maybe there was something weird about me. Maybe I had this kind of treatment coming. Maybe I was doing something to deserve it.

After awhile it seemed that the bully and I developed an unspoken agreement. I knew that I was going to be brutalized. He knew that I knew and simply waited for the right opportunity.

The velocity of life increased every time he picked on me and I realized that most of my thinking was directed toward figuring out how to avoid him.

And some days I did. I would actually go one entire, long summer's day without an encounter, though the fear was always there. The bully might take a day off but my alert mechanism stayed on the job. It would be nice looking back to think that I woke up one morning and said I'd had enough. One of those epiphanies when hell yawned and I felt its hot breath. But it wasn't really like that. It just kind of happened.

It was in the fall during a school grounds game of flag football.

Each kickoff was an opportunity for Wayne to run me over at full speed. On pass plays he followed me instead of the guy who caught the ball. During plays from scrimmage, he ignored the runner and simply ran into me on the pretext of blocking me out of the action, no matter where I was on the field.

No coaches or PE instructors were around to observe that Wayne was far more interested in harassing me than playing the game. Their only presence was the sound of conversation and occasional laughter coming from inside the gym.

So Wayne would knock me down with such violence that I was bleeding from several places less than halfway through the game. As the opposing team was getting ready to kick off again, a friend said to me. "He's going to run you down again, Buddy." I shook my head side to side and said, "Not this time." At least I think that's what I said. I know at least I thought it.

Let me switch to the present tense for a moment to better convey to you the full impact of what happened next:

The teams face off thirty or so yards apart and I make eye contact with Wayne. I stand up straight and motion for him to come on, waving to him maniacally, challenging him, taunting him, even giving him my best glare.

The kicker launches the ball into the air.

The other players on both sides angle away from the two of us, now running full speed toward each other. Getting closer and closer, twenty boys are now focused on us and not the football. Nobody even noticed the boy who caught the kickoff.

As we get closer I can clearly see that Wayne is red faced and contorted with anger, churning the ground, digging hard, building up enough momentum and speed to injure me badly. I try not to focus on that now. I avoid looking directly into his eyes as his frightening bulk gets closer to me.

At fifteen yards I pull up just a bit to motion him on, waving with both hands. Wayne's face gets even redder. He hesitates, then charges across the final yards running like a bull toward a red cape masquerading as gym shorts. At this moment, for Wayne, I cease to be a person and become simply a skinny, 120-pound irritant to be dealt with.

What happens next remains to this day the most perfect timing of any physical act I've ever attempted. Astonishingly, my spontaneous plan actually works.

At a distance I would guess to be no more than two or three yards I suddenly slide baseball style but a little more balled up, directly at his feet.

In this very short space he can't change direction. He can only hit my coiled and somewhat protected body, tripping over me at full speed. With a quick glance behind and above me I can see Wayne, all 240 howling pounds of him, airborne and starting to flip over onto his back.

He lands hard. Everyone there hears what sounds like a belly flop in a swimming pool. Except the surface we're on is hard packed dirt with a few patches of grass. There are not many visible places on his body that are not scraped and bleeding and undoubtedly some I can't see.

He lies there for a short time with no one even asking how he is. Then he slowly gets up and begins chasing me for fifteen minutes. The flag football game is over and a new, far more interesting game has begun. I easily stay just out of his reach and I wonder why I didn't use my greater speed and agility before.

The Physical Education instructor comes to the gym door, whistles us in and I am once again safely in an adult supervised environment as I change clothes and just barely let myself think of the inevitable consequence of my actions.

Just as I envisioned it he approaches me after the bell rings. I am resigned to what will undoubtedly be the most violent behavior that Wayne has ever directed my way. And I don't even care. Not after what I saw. It will almost be worth it.

I said to him, "you had that coming, you know you did."

To his credit, if you can credit a bully, he doesn't beat me up. Instead, he apologizes for treating me the way he had over the past six months or so and tells me he absolutely respected what I did.

"You're right, Buddy. I had that coming," he says.

The next day Wayne asks me to join his high school fraternity. The other guys playing ball with me that day never look at me the same way again. On graduation day I get some knowing looks and a few minor head nods as I head up for my diploma.

That's it. I manage to avoid a monumental ass kicking and the bully repents. A classic Hollywood ending that just happens to be true. But here is where the movie stops and gets rewound on the projector (remember, this is an old movie). We start back at the beginning and play it through in slow motion. What you see now is that everything I did was wrong. Everything.

I suffered in silence. I never told my parents, teachers or coaches. I never shared the pain with my friends. Even when there were witnesses and sometimes co-victims I held back from talking about it. And worst of all I played to his strength. Literally. I took him on in his own physically violent arena.

Two things made that situation possible. One, I got lucky and you can't count on luck when it comes to a bully. Two, Wayne still had something in him, some thread of humanity that responded to my desperate act. And you definitely don't want to count on that, either.

The good news is that school principals, teachers, counselors and coaches are far more on the alert today. Parents are hopefully more attuned to the bully problem, too. For the most part, the whole world is more enlightened. There are more places to turn.

The less than good news is that Today's Bully has evolved, too. And there's a good chance that he or she is more dangerous than ever with a lot more weapons at hand.

Today's Bullies may carry a weapon of some sort, even a gun. They may be in a gang. They may have a technically savvy clique that attacks other kids on social media. They may spread lies and rumors and hatred throughout the school environment and beyond with the flick of the SEND button.

Go up against today's bullies and they're likely to retaliate in a way that Wayne, limited to his own bulk and fists, could never have imagined.

Today, the action I finally took, which gave me an undeniable sense of redemption and made my dad so proud when I finally told him about it, could be a gateway to horror.

That's why this book is not about stories. It's about giving you and your children the clear information and the tools needed to help navigate the bullying experience that, if it's not facing you now, is very likely on its way. Because the unfortunate truth is, when it comes to Today's Bully, it's generally not *if*, it's *when*.

# *Preface*

# "Just Tell Me What to Do..."

THE BREVITY AND CONCISENESS of this book represent a planned and very conscious decision. Too much of the same or similar information and too many choices can sometimes lead to confusion and immobilization. Our knowledge of bullying doesn't have to be encyclopedic. Our response to it doesn't need to be complicated. But it does need to be thoughtful and cautious.

The thing to keep in mind about bullying is that we already know the threat. Educators, journalists, parents, forward-thinking law enforcement officials, elected officials, members of the clergy and a storm of media coverage have all focused on bullying and the troubling and dangerous trends that surround it.

We don't need any more convincing. Our attention is aroused.

Within that context we want to remind you again that the words you are reading are not a re-interpretation of the growing number of psychological and sociological studies carried out to provide insight into the causes of bullying behavior. And these pages won't provide you with the latest law enforcement compendium about youth violence, which also is expanding.

There is ample literature, with lengthy research and highly documented studies devoted to examining the trends in contemporary bullying behavior. This book will not add to that particular body of knowledge.

What it will do is provide a road map, or in keeping with the evolution of bullying itself, a GPS that will help readers navigate a world in which bullying has been transformed from something more akin to an unfortunate rite of passage into a serous public health concern.

"Just tell me what to do," is the theme of this helpful guide published by the National Center for the Prevention of Community Violence. It's a theme we set forth now and promise to stay with. It's a theme that carries with it the tools and resources you need to feel informed, empowered and prepared to deal with the problem immediately and decisively.

**"Popular culture is a powerful force.**
**We can't make it go away.**
**The best we can do is try to understand it.**
**Then help our children navigate it."**

Part of that preparation requires an honest look at the forces in play. For example, the epidemic of bullying coincides with an epidemic of gang membership in America, a 40% surge according to the FBI's National Gang Threat Assessment study that stunned law enforcement officials across the country.

Without connecting any dots in a cause and effect relationship, the fact is that our children have the cult of dominance and the allure of the thug life marketed to them every day in music, video games, television, movies, social media, and clothing.

Popular culture, fueled by mass and highly personalized media, is a powerful force. We can't make it go away. The best we can do is try to understand it. Then help our children navigate it.

Back to gangs for a moment, it's worth noting that the big league gangs have minor league farm teams. And many of their best recruits can be found among Today's Bullies.

Father Gregory Boyle, founder of Homeboy Industries in Los Angeles and a leading advocate for young people involved in gangs, addressed a Virginia gathering in May 2012. His words echo today.

"Hopeful kids….don't join gangs," Father Boyle offers. "There has never been, in the history of the world, a hopeful child who joins a gang," said the priest who has for three decades made his life rescuing young people from Los Angeles' most brutal gangs.

"Our job, then, is to infuse hope," Father Boyle said.

This same wisdom and the power of hope that it supports are applicable in dealing with Today's Bully and the trail that he or she leaves behind.

There are many reasons young people try out bullying and a number of specific risk factors have been identified. But we suggest that one common denominator of an emerging bully, identical to the factors involved with the decision to join a gang, is that underlying lack of hope.

There is a desperate tone in the inner voice of a bully—that there is no hope in fitting in — so why not gain acceptance through dominance? If you perceive that you aren't being allowed into the circle, then punish those who you believe are keeping you out. And all too often, there's no one there with an alternative.

Our job then, is to infuse hope.

As adults, we need to show the hopeless that there is a better way, fill the voids that created the behavior and help the bully find the better angel within. But that's only after we've helped provide for or otherwise support the safety of the victim.

And that's what constitutes a best practice when it comes to bullying. Perhaps *the* best practice.

# The Culture of Bullying — What Is It Really About and Why Are So Many Young People Embracing It?

EVERYONE IS WATCHING. A live audience and millions of national television and on-line viewers are looking on as the announcement is made that singer-songwriter Taylor Swift has won the MTV Video Music Award for Best Female Video. Immediately, Kanye West defiantly invades the stage to grab the award from a shocked Swift as a protest to his perception that she is undeserving. According to MTV News, the crowd is silent and confused. They don't know how to respond.

This startling scene from pop culture left an indelible image that cannot be forgotten by the large numbers of people who saw it. Or can it? Kanye West is still a highly successful music artist, fashion designer, film director and world-class tweeter. In fact, he's probably even more popular after the incident.

While we can't blame artists like Kanye and his followers for the myriad reasons why kids bully, we can certainly propose that for many young people the impact of teen culture speaks loudly to the attitude of defiance and domination.

In much of today's society, to be crude, inappropriate, mean spirited, rude and socially unacceptable is now grounds for some type of celebratory award in its own right. The sense of human entitlement and domination has clearly made a dent in, and in some instances even replaced, the ideal of civility.

What was once thought of as an insult or "put down," a big part of traditional bullying, has now evolved into an overall and consistent "in your face" style of behavior strongly supported by a number of Fortune 500 media giants and sold as "youth or pop culture."

**"It becomes impossible to tell which came first, the anger or the marketing of the anger."**

This phenomenon was well defined in the PBS Frontline documentary *The Merchants of Cool* featuring media correspondent Douglas Rushkoff. He alluded to what we are seeing as the rise of Today's Bully when he declared that youth culture and media culture are now one and the same, and it becomes impossible to tell "which came first, the anger or the marketing of the anger."

With the backing of the extensive empire of wealth that supports youth culture, the new style of bullying behavior rarely occurs in isolation. It operates within a context that is supported by the entertainment and fashion industries, professional sports, politics, corporate America and more. The victims of the behavior may at times feel that their abusers are part of society in general, not simply the negative choices and aberrant behaviors of select individuals.

Moreover, bullies today easily feed on peer pressure. That pressure, when combined with the power of popular culture, can sometimes be interpreted as a license to insult, abuse and injure without consideration of the consequences.

These behaviors, which include dismissals, exclusivity, put downs, profanity, threats, and even physical violence may not even be seen as bullying, but rather a normal part of their existence, and in some cases, a means to survival in the growing "in your face" world.

Those of us who have worked in an office or other work setting understand the penalties for creating a hostile workplace. Why aren't these same "hostile work environment" rules applied in other public and private places?

**"The rule book and the whistle need to be put back into the game."**

So how do children and teens escape this new form of abuse?

At one tragic extreme, some have ended their lives. For others, reactions range from depression to acting out.

Finally, for some, they escape by transforming into a bully themselves.

We face relentless pressure that this behavior is the "new normal." The bullying culture has become so prevalent and dominant that we feel reduced to bystanders.

To extend a sports analogy, the rulebook and the whistle need to be put back into the game. This need comes from set expectations of behavior and stated sanctions for those who do not abide by those expectations in places where we have a say — at home, in school, in the workplace, in recreational and competitive sports and in our neighborhoods.

The scope is difficult to get our arms around. The State of New York announced a 2011 survey of high school students that showed 18% of them reported being bullied on school property in 2010 and 16% reported being bullied electronically. That's more than one third of students reporting a bullying experience. And of course, that doesn't take into account what's not reported.

# Bullying Defined

A DICTIONARY DEFINITION FROM more than fifty years ago describes a bully as "harsh" and "cruel," someone who is "habitually threatening to others." After half a century the words still ring true.

According to most contemporary definitions, bullying occurs when a person is exposed repeatedly to "negative actions" on the part of one or more other persons.

These "negative actions" refer to one person intentionally inflicting injury or discomfort upon another person, through physical contact, through words, or in other ways.

# How Bullying Got Out of Control

CHILDREN ARE BULLYING EACH other in frighteningly effective 21st century ways. These are not your father's bullies. Armed with social media and supported by a culture that seems to glorify bullying throughout a wide spectrum of activities, today's kids experience bullying behavior in every direction they turn.

**"Many parents are numb to bullying because they experience it every day at work."**

Many parents are either numb to bullying or far less sensitive than they should be because they may experience it every day at work. The bullies of their own childhood have grown up and become their co-workers and supervisors.

Too often it seems that the least compassionate and most domineering get ahead.

Some would say it's always been that way, that the media has simply expanded and amplified the nastiness.

Our history lends some truth to that assertion through political campaigns that introduced us to contentious behavior and outright ugly moments shortly after America declared its independence. The earliest days of the republic also saw intimidation and domineering behavior incorporated into military training and discipline.

In fact, there is substantial historical record to suggest that the very people who sacrificed so much to escape harassment in the old world, brought bullies along with them. Of course what happened in the slave ships and in the aftermath of their arrival on our shores took bullying to levels of inhumanity.

But while the historical record bears witness to intense and excessive examples of bullying over the years, never before has there been a time when 7.3 million children in America have a parent in the penal system. Or when 1,400,000 youths claim gang affiliation. Or when countless handguns are available even to small children. Never has there been an opportunity to bully a child so brutally using nothing but a cell phone. Things have become different, and they've become more serious.

What we can safely say is that bullying evolved to the place where we find it today and it serves little purpose to explore exactly how it arrived. What matters is that it's here.

Hostility is commonplace.

Look at our political process. Much of our television broadcasting is filled with negative, angry, name-calling political ads that seek an attack platform instead of common ground. In many local and regional races, where there's less oversight, these candidates don't just want to win an election. They want to destroy their opponent.

Our kids digest this behavior as part of a steady diet.

Incredibly, the news media gave a little ho-hum back page coverage to the October 2011 revelation by the FBI that membership in gangs has increased 40% in just two years as the national economic picture declined and more young people gave up on the idea of being a contributing member of a society that leaves them out.

Ho hum.

But let some of those expanding numbers of gang members take each other out, and even more newsworthy, do some collateral damage in a drug related shootout, and it's a different story. One that actually gets some coverage.

Our news media now puts its 24/7 offerings together on the news placement priority of "if it bleeds it leads," an approach deemed more likely to attract the less than attentive eyes of most viewers. Or worse, even the media gets jaded with so much violence and manages to transform some celebrity divorce or the latest update from the people in a reality TV show into a major story despite the domestic war zone going on all over America.

Thoughtful and more in-depth journalistic coverage is threatened as newspapers collapse. The majority of people now get their news almost exclusively from the TV, the Internet or even smaller screens. And all the while, the once solid line between news and entertainment continues to blur.

The whole phenomenon of human nature devolving under pressure brings to mind the "Lord of the Flies" by Nobel Prize-winning author William Golding. Now mostly relegated to high school literature classes, the insightful and very topical work tells the story of a group of British boys stuck on a deserted island who try to govern themselves, with disastrous results.

**"The vacuum left behind by absent parents and home lives where empathy is unknown, supervision is absent and moral compasses are unavailable"**

At an allegorical level, the novel is a study in conflicting human impulses: to embrace civilization, live its rules, peacefully and in harmony, or, to live simply guided by the desire for power and the will to dominate.

Themes include the tension between groupthink and individuality, between rational and emotional reactions, and between morality and immorality. The narrative carries the story of how these juxtaposed impulses play out, and how the different characters respond.

There is something of "Lord of the Flies" inherent in the gang and youth violence crisis in America and in the vacuum left behind by absent parents and home lives where empathy is unknown, supervision is rare or absent and moral compasses are either unavailable or considered a luxury not to be sought. This mentality, fueled as we discussed by the combination of news and entertainment industries, helps smother neighborhoods, then schools, then our children.

As authors we began our journey piecing together examples of best practices and stories of hope from across America and the world in our 2012 release "***No COLORS — 100 Ways To Stop Gangs from Taking Over Our Communities.***"

As we turn our attention to the similar yet distinctive bullying crisis, it is clear that whatever measures we can take to protect our children will require a multi-pronged campaign. And that includes a demand for changes within the business community, from elected officials, school authorities and, perhaps most especially, the individuals and the collective industry that controls not just what is marketed to our children but the tone with which it's promoted.

That's a very tall order indeed, but we have to start somewhere. That's why we advocate for what most good athletic programs or events do to maintain an acceptable level of civility and in most sports, that means a whistle. Bullying in every venue will continue until someone "blows the whistle," stops the play, and assesses a penalty before the game resumes.

We need to offer a set of rules.

And we need to give out those whistles to as many people as possible.

Because bullying does not just happen in one venue.

Children have been exposed to bullying since the dawn of recorded time. But while past generations were bullied in various settings most of it didn't come complete with bullies who carry guns, travel in gangs or have a multitude of willing and tech-savvy followers who have become adept at character assassination through social media.

So, begin here — stand at the starting line of developing empathy for a generation of kids under pressure. Have that empathy both for the bullies and the victims.

And let's open our hearts to solutions, which need to be applied throughout the school, the community, and in your own home. It is with this understanding that we begin.

And remember that our "whistles" are good anywhere.

# Let's Dispel the Myths About Bullying

### MYTH. Bullying is a simple school issue.

The gang crisis got out of control because we kept trying to solve it as a police problem, not a community-wide crisis. The same is true in bullying. As long as we think the schools alone can fix it, we'll never make headway.

### MYTH. Bullying is a rite of passage for kids.

The old phrase, "Kids will just be kids" is also aiding the spread of uncivil behavior within our communities. To believe that bullying is simply part of growing up is a great mistake. Bullying is an act of violence and treating it as anything less is an obstacle to improving the situation.

### MYTH. Today's bullies really aren't all that different from when you were in school.

The understanding that bullies in today's society are very different from your experience-based perception can be helped along by answering the following question: Did you know of anyone from your school or neighborhood who committed suicide due to the impact of bullying while you were growing up? Tragedies such as these are occurring daily in this new world. Today's bullies have graduated from name-calling to cyber threats and gang intimidation and we have failed as a society to understand their new and potentially deadly weapons.

### MYTH. Verbal and physical abuse is nothing more than a simple bullying incident.

When we place ongoing verbal abuse and even physical abuse under the classification of bullying, we allow for increased victimization within our society. Many people fail to look at bullying as a violation of existing legal statutes. Many of the incidents we pass off as bullying are, in fact, against the law. When these instances occur and are not addressed, we give people a license to continue their negative, anti-social and possibly illegal behavior.

### MYTH. Ignore bullying and believe it will go away.

This social problem, without intervention, is unlikely to heal itself. Individual bullies, not unlike nations that exhibit bullying behavior on a global scale, exist on power and they are not very quick to give that away. Believing that ignoring their actions hoping they will stop is usually not advised. In most cases, we urge immediate response and action.

### MYTH. Encourage the victim to stand up and fight back.

Physical engagement of a bully is not advised. This may have been the reaction of choice for past generation but it carries a much greater risk today as the weapons and the potential for retaliation have changed. We also recommend that bystanders protest verbally when possible but not enter a physical bullying situation — rather, call for help, recruit support from others and verbally protest the abuse.

### MYTH. Cyberbullying is just mean kids acting out in social media.

That may be true, but this new media is incredibly powerful and broad in scope. The choice by some adults to minimize their own exposure to social media has served to increase the potential for younger people to be victimized through social networking. While we may not be able to block this particular avenue to bullying, more education directed to parents and community stakeholders can make a positive difference.

### MYTH. Kids get their ideas from each other. Bullying is not stimulated by parents and role models.

Our nation's contentious political arena plays a role. The unchecked intentional injuring of opposing players in professional sports plays a role.

These role models for bullying are all there, in our cultural DNA.

Bullies exist in every part of our society and in order for us to find the appropriate solutions, we must also agree to address this as a social issue in general and not just a concern facing kids in school.

# Understand All Five Traditional Forms of Bullying

### Isolation

Many of us can remember not being invited to a party or social function. We may also remember days when we were not picked for the kickball team or maybe sat alone at the lunch table. Part of this behavior may be due to the normal developmental insensitivity that many children exhibit toward their peers. But purposeful social isolation and the ongoing attempt to separate and intentionally exclude individuals should be seen as a viable weapon in the bully's arsenal.

### Put downs

When someone made fun of us by making comments about the way we dressed, or possibly our actions in a given situation, it hurt. It still does.

### Name-calling

Labeling one another is often a kind of short hand for how we organize the world. But continuously substituting someone's real name with some sort of critical label or nickname has an emotionally painful impact that bullies understand all too well.

### Taunting

Taunting with its ongoing attack and intimidation elements is a powerful bully's tool. It can take place through inflammatory text messages, social media or through close physical proximity to the bully.

### Ongoing Physical Contact

Bullying is rarely about a single incident, the shove delivered unseen in the school corridor, the fight that resolves the issue or any single physical encounter. Bullying is far more related to patterns. And those patterns often become escalated, leading to the potential for serious physical harm.

# At What Age Does Bullying Become a Danger to Kids?

WHILE BULLYING CAN OCCUR even in the pre-school period of a child's life, it often reaches its peak when most boys are at puberty and trying to impress the girls who have reached that point an average of two years earlier. While some studies show that the direct physical assault aspect of bullying peaks in the middle school or early high school years and then declines, the verbal abuse aspect appears to remain relatively constant.

**"There is a willingness to try out being mean."**

In many cases, there is a willingness to "try out" being mean among both girls and boys. Both have discovered new powers but do not have an owner's manual on how to use them. In fact, the 21st century dominance culture seems to demand that young people road test some of the relationship notions (and of course, bullying itself is a form of dysfunctional relationship) they recently acquired.

We call it the "landing" of the culture. Our society trains and promotes dominant and aggressive behavior and by middle school it's looking for a place to touch down.

"Shall I be civil or uncivil?" is the decision at hand.

By the time these kids enter high school, the decision has usually been made.

The good news is that the decision need not be permanent; nor does it need to result in overwhelming sanctions. But it needs to be exposed, counseled, monitored and made accountable if it doesn't stop.

The best anecdote is teaching your child empathy by role modeling, beginning as early as possible. Exhibit a sincere caring for others, an absence of malace, a love for animals and nature and at every opportunity, explain the empathetic action to your kids when they see it happening. Kids pay attention.

Teaching assertiveness is also advised. For example, when another child says, "those are the ugliest shoes I have even seen" — the assertive response would be, "That's not nice. You shouldn't speak to other people that way."

# Between Meanness and Bullying

**Both meanness and bullying** can involve an imbalance of power between the bully and victim with that imbalance including both social class and physical differences. But meanness has a subjective component and what one person perceives as mean or even cruel behavior may be more the result of underdeveloped social skills and unintentional slights on the part of the perpetrator.

The key difference seems to be frequency, and the intent to control. A bully seeks to make another submissive to his or her power, through social, psychological and physical aggression.

Bullying is a relationship in which one individual seeks to gain power and control over the life of another.

Most experts agree that the behavior becomes "bullying" when it is frequent and intentional.

**"The key difference seems to be
not only the frequency
but the intent to control."**

Bullying is repeated and frequent intentional actions that bring harm to an individual.

# What Bullying and Gangs Have in Common

| **BULLIES** | **GANG MEMBERS** |
|---|---|
| Want recognition | Want recognition |
| Love "the show" | Love "the show" |
| Don't mind hurting others | Don't mind hurting others |
| Like strength in numbers* | Like strength in numbers * |
| Seek dominance | Seek dominance |
| Disrespect authority | Disrespect authority |
| Want to be admired | Want to be admired |
| Often pay a heavy price as adult | Often pay a heavy price as adult |

* But bullies also act alone, one-on-one

# "JUST TELL ME WHAT TO DO..."

**A Compilation of Suggested Solutions to Bullying Situations Parents, Teachers, Coaches and Family Members Will Encounter**

# Preparing Our Children For Bullying Encounters

# Leave Nothing Unsaid with Your Child, Have Regular "Bully Talks"

**One of the first** things we should observe is our children's relationship with their friends.

If you don't see any interaction with classmates or neighborhood kids, this could be an open message that your child is struggling socially.

If your child does have frequent interaction with friends, part of your discussion with him or her should include the suggestion to step up for those kids who seem isolated.

Suggest to your child that he or she might have lunch with the kid who sits alone in the cafeteria. Reducing this social isolation is a strong antidote to bullying. If you're told that such an action may be in violation of unspoken clique rules, it's also time to include that notion that your kid may be in the wrong clique as part of the talk.

Research tells us that children really do look to parents and caregivers for advice and help on tough decisions. Sometimes spending 15 minutes a day talking can reassure kids that they can talk to their parents if they have a problem.

Start conversations about daily life and feelings with questions like these:

What was one good thing that happened today? Any bad things?

What is lunchtime like at your school? Who do you sit with? What do you talk about?

If applicable, what is it like to ride the school bus?

When it comes time for some direct talk about bullies, you might want to consider the following conversation starters:

What does "bullying" mean to you?

Describe what kids who bully are like. Why do you think people bully?

Who are the adults you trust most when it comes to things like bullying?

Have you ever felt scared to go to school because you were afraid of bullying?

What ways have you tried to change it?

What do you think parents can do to help stop bullying?

Have you or your friends left other kids out on purpose? Do you think that was bullying? Why or why not?

What do you usually do when you see bullying going on?

Do you ever see kids at your school being bullied by other kids? How does it make you feel?

Have you ever tried to help someone who is being bullied? What happened? What would you do if it happens again?

In spite of our best efforts, our children, especially our teenagers, don't always tell us about their lives.

**"Once your child enters middle school years, the real dangers begin."**

We suggest that these important communications occur early in school life and that they continue throughout your kids' secondary school career.

Younger children are more likely to enjoy storytelling about their day. Get a pulse on their activities. Let your child know that you are interested and actively paying attention to what is going on in his or her life.

Teenagers often require a more subtle touch. They typically resist too much parental supervision in general and inquiry in particular. But these conversations are critical and the earlier they start the better. Once your child enters middle school years, and even before, the real dangers begin as Today's Bully begins to use social media and network with older, more physically developed kids.

# Making the Distinction Between Self-Esteem and Selfish Esteem

THIS ISSUE IS WELL articulated by Jon Siebels, the Guitarist of Eve 6, in his blog on the Huffington Post, "School Bullying: To End It, We Must Change Our Culture."

"When I think of bullies," Siebels writes, "the first thing that comes to my mind is that a bully is someone who is overcompensating for low self-esteem or self-worth; however, studies have suggested that the opposite is true."

**"In the corporate world people throw their fellow employees under the bus to get a promotion, and at our schools kids harass each other for being different."**

In the '80s and '90s there was a big push for parents to promote self-esteem in their kids. Have we taken this too far? Are we teaching our kids that believing in oneself has to come at the expense of belittling others? Is this what they are learning by the way that we treat others?

"Dictionary.com has two definitions of 'self-esteem.' The first is 'respect for or a favorable opinion of oneself,' and the second is 'an unduly high opinion of oneself; vanity,' he observes.

"The second definition seems to be the more accurate one today. The term should probably be changed to 'selfish-esteem.' "

"We'll do whatever it takes to make ourselves appear in a more favorable light. Just take a look at message boards across the net. There is an unbelievable amount of hate being posted on these sites. In our political races the candidate who wins is the one who makes his opponent look the worst. In professional sports, teams are dominated by one or two power players. In the corporate world people throw their fellow employees under the bus to get a promotion, and at our schools kids harass each other for being different," Siebels notes.

Instill self-esteem, but also make your children aware of the dangers of letting their real sense of self worth get knocked out of the way by too much selfish ambition.

# The Potential Impact of Bullying

MAKE BULLYING A SERIOUS issue with your children. It's a potentially dangerous world and they need to know why you are attentive and concerned. And you should be. All of us should be because the stakes are high and the following consequences could be part of the experience:

- Depression
- Physical ailments (headaches, stomach aches, ulcers)
- Sleep problems
- Academic problems
- Frequent switching of schools
- Low self-esteem
- Weight loss or gain
- Long-term emotional scars
- Serious physical injury
- Property damage (possibly to your home)
- Problems with future relationships
- Violent revenge, aggression
- Suicide

# Ten Suggestions To Help Your Child Navigate Around the Bullies

1. Work at understanding your child better. And it can take "work" in the form of giving more of your time, especially in the listening mode.
2. Get control of social media. You pay for it; you own it. Kids need to know they are being observed.
3. Have a reasonable idea about the popular culture that impacts your children. It's the water they swim in and you should have more than a passing sense of what's involved. You don't have to try to defeat it. That would be a futile effort at best. And you certainly don't want to adopt it as yours in one of those uncomfortable attempts to be a friend instead of a parent. Just know what's out there that is surrounding your child in peer groups, at school and in the confines of his or her room.
4. Know your child's friends. Spend time talking with them in your home or in public places.
5. Do your best to know, even on a minimal level, the parents and siblings of your child's friend.

6. Model non-conflict behavior in front of your child. Demonstrating a spirit of cooperation will not only be beneficial for children who observe it, but also for those practicing it.
7. Make every effort to help your child feel independently strong, confident and capable without first requiring them to see themselves as either an oppressed person or an oppressor.
8. Have specific expectations of your child's school.
9. Have specific expectations of those who work with your child — including educational professionals and paraprofessionals and anyone in a position of responsibility or mentoring.
10. Be aware that some kids give up because the tunnel is too dark. Pay close attention to this sense in your child and support him or her in recognizing it in friends or acquaintances.

# The Bully. The Victim. The Bystander. Why Bystanders Have the Power

On its most basic and potentially most harmful level, bullying is a deliberate, direct attack on the human spirit.

Most bullying is done with an audience. Bullies seek cultural rewards in the new world of Today's Bully so well modeled for them in the media.

They seek a stage. If you don't open the curtain as audience, Act One never happens.

To extend the theater analogy a bit, there are generally three roles involved in a bullying situation:

The bully. The victim. The bystander(s).

From the perspective of statistics, it is far more likely that your child will be a bystander than a victim or a bully.

So the response of the bystander is a key to affecting the way the rest of the drama gets played out. If bystanders reject the bullying situation, call for it to stop, they are refusing to be an audience and bear witness to what the bully is attempting to do. That refusal can be a powerful force of change for all three of the players.

If you teach young people to recognize injustice, then you have a far better chance to move toward justice. It should be everyone's sense of duty to stand up for someone being abused.

**"The many stand up for the few."**

In most cases, the reaction of bystanders changes everything for the bully. If the others call for it to stop, standing up for the victim, it removes the social reward from the bully.

This powerful sense of solidarity also elevates the self-esteem of those who step in and change the social dynamic.

Suddenly, not only has bullying ceased, but the kids who acted are the new heroes for the moment. New friendships can be forged or at the very least, a greater sense of tolerance. The many stand up for the few. The bully does not get the respect or fear he or she wants. Removing that reward can even have the affect of helping the bullying child change his or her behavior.

**"The bystander is the key for stopping this behavior."**

The nations of Scandinavia have learned that the bystander is the key to stopping this behavior in their schools and in their communities. The creators of the KiVa program, now being implemented throughout schools in Finland, puts the behavior of the bystander at the center of their anti-bullying strategy. KiVa is named from the Finnish *kiusaamista vastaan*, meaning "against bullying" and *kiva*, meaning "nice."

Their programs focus on daily encouragement of empathy and standing up for others. And their results are highly positive. They are successfully on the way toward eliminating or significantly restricting bullying behavior in their school environments.

Empathy can go to both the victim and the bully. Let the bully know they don't have to be mean to get attention.

We **do not** recommend physical intervention.

Just as adults evaluate how to intervene in a potentially violent situation, kids need to make the same careful choices.

Gauge the situation. If a kid is being physically harmed, is it advisable to step in and break up the fight without creating the opportunity for more harm? That is a situation that may be difficult to determine for an adult, much less a young child. As a result, intervening physically should be an absolute last resort.

Consider verbal intervention only. Voice disapproval of the situation.

"Please stop." "Don't do that."

If there is more than one bystander, send someone for help.

Along with personal example, one of the best ways to develop empathy in young people is to encourage regular community service.

**"Empathy in your child is a learned response."**

Service outside the walls of a school or other organization is not only becoming a prerequisite for application to many colleges, it's a very direct and meaningful way for kids to see the world beyond their home. You can help them get involved through places of places of worship, Boys & Girls Clubs, with the Food Bank, food kitchens or other social services within your community. Many high schools now have mandatory community service requirements, but it never hurts to add on another.

Developing empathy in your child is a learned response. Model it. Show compassion for the victims of everyday life around the world or those less fortunate in our own neighborhoods. Cultivate community service. Cultivate the sense of empathy and caring for those carrying a heavier load than your family.

Lee Hirsch, the producer of the film *Bully*, released in 2012, said in a Huffington Post interview that the organization he is founding is creating "a fantastic curriculum with youth leadership facilitation guides. There is a whole model for how to best engage with the film. We want to see whole schools facilitating social action campaigns!"

Hirsch reinforced an important element to the problem: teaching kids the powerful, positive impact of empathy.

"What excites me is the broader potential of thousands of kids making the decision to be empathetic and understanding the impact of their choices of how they treat people -- which will have life-long positive repercussions."

Hirsch's movie promotion includes the powerful call to action: "It's Time to Take a Stand."

# Rehearse for the Show, Use Role Play to Practice Reactions to Bullying

The KiVa strategy developed in Finland is based on a primary theory of empowering the bystander to effectively but safely intervene in the bullying situation. They make heroes of the kids who step in appropriately. They role-play, frequently discussing and acting out bystander responses to bullying scenarios. They champion the fact that respect belongs to everybody. And it's working, probably better than any other recognized program in the world.

In Finland, they have long recognized that the bystander makes or breaks the bullying stage play.

## Intervening in a Bullying Situation

Those witnessing a bullying event must first evaluate the safety of the situation: if there are weapons involved or other threats of physical harm, the bystander should notify a professional to intervene.

It cannot be said enough that stepping in physically is an absolute last resort and should never be recommended to a child. The most likely result is placing another child in harm's way.

Otherwise, bystanders can help by:

- Telling the bully that what he or she is doing is wrong
- Inviting the victim to leave the situation with them
- Not laughing or otherwise encouraging the bully
- Talking to the victim in private and conveying support
- Including the victim in their activities and/or helping that individual avoid other potential bullying situations
- Avoiding spreading rumors about what happened

Victor Schwartz, M.D., medical director for The Jed Foundation, said this in a press release on the mental health impact of bullying:

"The bully is often harassing the victim to demonstrate power and entertain the bystanders. If those bystanders laugh or encourage the bully, the situation is likely to continue. However, if the bystanders are sympathetic to the victim, then the bully loses influence and his or her reason for bullying. Therefore, it's important for bystanders to recognize the power they have to stop the bullying situation and make it known that this type of behavior is not acceptable."

Young people who stand by without offering assistance on some level while another kid is bullied can carry away emotional scars from that experience just as the victim might.

Elementary school children often move through the school in groups and there's less likely to be a situation of extreme isolation. There is usually more opportunity for bystanders to react together to stop the bully.

## There are reasons why children choose not to intervene

- They fear they can make the matter worse.
- They fear the immediate threat of becoming the next victim.

- They are evaluating whether or not the victim deserves it.

Discuss situational responses with your children. Coach them not to intervene physically.

What would they do if a group of bullies were attacking a friend?

Or another child they didn't know.

What would you do? Would your child be afraid of being labeled a tattler or a snitch? What do you think the teacher would do?

By exploring these questions with your son or daughter, it will help them pre-think such situations and be more likely to take an effective step when the time comes.

Even if kids want to stop the bullying, they may not know how to handle it.

Here are some suggestions on coaching your son or daughter on how to handle an observation that a school child is being bullied:

Spend time with individuals being bullied at school. Talk with them, sit with them at lunch, or share activities with them on school grounds or otherwise hang out together.

One of the most important aspects of this time together is the act of listening.

Call the child being bullied at home to encourage and offer advice. Do not use impersonal texting.

Tell a trusted adult, like a teacher or coach. Tell them in person or leave them a note.

Set a good example.

Send a message or go up after the event to the person who was bullied and say that what happened "wasn't cool and I'm here for you."

Look for opportunities to contribute to the anti-bullying culture of your school through creating posters, stories or films.

In discussing potential bystander responses with your high school-aged child, help your son or daughter realize that the situation and the potential to effectively intervene can be complicated and dangerous. The situation may involve kids at an age where the 21st century weapons may come into play, or organized bands of youth (members of a gang) gather to bully a single kid.

We suggest that if this happens bystanders should first contact any adult or authority possible.

Next, we suggest that you coach your child to gather as many other kids as possible and together provide the intervention. Send one for help. Gently and quietly protest verbally.

Make the discussion brief and directive. It's the right thing to do. No discussion about that.

Next, help the child move away from the situation and comfort the victim.

We suggest that the rescuers have their cell phones to their ears, hopefully with someone on the line, so the bullies perceive that help is on the way.

We do not suggest the children record video unless it can definitely be done without the bullies' knowledge. This could escalate the situation quickly.

Regardless, if your kid witnesses another child being bullied, make it clear that keeping mute is not an option. Be a responsible bystander and do everything carefully and thoughtfully. Most importantly, tell an adult, fast.

# Kids May Not Love Every Classmate, But They Understand Politeness

In our view, politeness, as it includes but goes beyond the "please" and "thank you" level is one of the most underutilized behaviors that adults can instill in and model for young people.

**"Kids 'get' polite."**

Even as early as the first grade, notes psychologist Dr. Lisa Damour in an April 10, 2012 discussion on the "Civic Commons" radio program in Cleveland, parents can help their children understand that in school, they may not like to play with some students as much as others, but they are expected to be polite to everyone.

**"Ultimately, it's the initial reaction to the bully that seems to determine whether or not it is continued."**

"Kids 'get' polite," Dr. Demour says. She explains that it not realistic to teach a utopian view that everyone should get along all the time and to like everyone.

In school, we need to remember that these kids are assigned to a class of children not of their choosing, from different home experiences and it's unrealistic to expect perfect behavior. But while a little forced socialization may not be perfect, it beats the alternative of none.

In addition, Dr. Demour notes, parents can help their children learn to be assertive and to stand up for themselves. Ultimately, it's the initial reaction to the bully that seems to determine whether or not it is continued and here, a bit of well-directed assertiveness is an excellent accompaniment to the politeness.

Adding some resilience to the mix is another good idea. Maureen Healy, MA, MBA writes on the subject of resilience in a piece entitled "Is Your Child Resilient?," created for "This Emotional Life," a PBS series designed to explore ways to improve social relationships and emotional issues.

In it she offers tips for cultivating resiliency in kids, a strength we feel is key to navigating the maze of bullying in school and in later life.

**Cultivate Optimism**—Become a parent who looks on the "bright side." As we become more optimistic in our thoughts, habits and eventually actions, you will show the way for your child to do the same.

**Focus on Strengths**—Children need to have a clear level of self-awareness regarding inner strengths, no matter what the world is reflecting to them. And as a parent, it helps to focus on those strengths and reinforce them.

In her 2012 book, "Growing Happy Kids: How to Foster Inner Confidence, Success and Happiness," Healy explains how to nurture this deeper type of strength (resilience) in children so they can move forward with positive expectations and see their potential, versus staying stuck in someone else's perspective.

Her suggestion is to keep nudging our children to see their strengths, develop them into skills and believe that things will work out for them, whether it is today, tomorrow, the next day or even further into the future.

**Openness to Change**—Kids who can "go with the flow" are developing a type of interpersonal flexibility that allows them to change, add new ideas and people into their life, subtract those things that aren't working as well and keep focused on their good, despite any current problems.

# Differences and Diversity Are Wonderful, but Avoid Social Isolation

Although Today's Bully has more weapons in his or her arsenal, the fact is that the explanations for why some young people turn to bullying are often the same as they've always been.

Unhappy or unfulfilled young people become bullies.

Or it's young people aspiring for a higher social status. Many teenagers focus on the present. They don't think about consequences. They don't think that their cruel words and actions can hurt others.

Labeling others is a good example, and unfortunately, it's rampant in social media. Children who express themselves outwardly as gay, lesbian, bisexual or transgender can have a particularly difficult time with social media stereotyping and labeling.

Even being particularly intelligent and successful in school can set your child apart from the pack; or coming from a more affluent — or less affluent -- home; or dressing differently than the majority of kids; or speaking a different primary language or being of mixed racial heritage.

No matter what the perceived difference is (generally on the part of the majority) different has the potential to create vulnerability.

When we gain a little more perspective in life, it's clear that being different can be a good thing. Individuality is something many people aspire to and value. But for young people in a school setting, different continues to be vulnerable and you may need to prepare your child for handling the possible, and even likely, bullying that may result.

**"If your kids are different and socially isolated, it's a classic formula for bullying."**

The best defense is confidence. Assure the young person that he or she has every right to be accepted as everyone else.

Encourage the young person to pick their friends carefully and cultivate close, meaningful relationships.

If your kid is perceived as being different and socially isolated, it's a classic formula for bullying. Bullies pick out the more demure, the loner, the isolated one, the one set apart.

The sense of being set apart can take on a different flavor when it's done with a bit of confidence. Confidence building in your child can be developed or enhanced through a number of activities, including the arts, sports, community service and anything else that offers focus and a sense of achievement and camaraderie. Each of these and other activities can help a young person become more self-actualized and take pride in who they are and what they accomplish.

Each has the potential to promote self-esteem, provide a positive after-school activity and, in the right circumstances, cultivate a network of friends who share the same interests.

**Understand the special risks faced by LGBT young people.**

The term "ostracize" goes back to ancient Greece, the word coming from *ostracon,* a small piece of a broken pot used as a ballot in voting to banish or exile a certain member of the community.

Citizen peers would cast their vote by writing the name of the person on the piece of pottery; the vote was counted and if unfavorable the person was generally exiled for a period of ten years from the city, thus giving rise to the term "ostracism."

Kids today don't use shards of pottery. They use cell phones, exclusion, name-calling and character assassination. But the result is the same — the fundamental removal of that person from the clique, the club, and the group of chosen ones. And this exile may last longer than the decade favored by the early Greeks. It may last a lifetime. And in some cases it may make that lifetime all too short.

According to the Suicide Prevention Resource Center, lesbian, gay, bi-sexual and transgender youth attempt suicide at a rate 2–4 times higher than that of their heterosexual peers.

In the words of one expert, LGBT adolescents "must cope with developing a sexual minority identity in the midst of negative comments, jokes, and often the threat of violence because of their sexual orientation and/or transgender identity."

A recent review of the research identified 19 studies linking suicidal behavior in lesbian, gay, and bisexual adolescents to bullying at school, especially among young people with "cross-gender appearance, traits, or behaviors."

The Suicide Prevention Resource Center notes that it is often the children most at risk for suicide who are bullied, which in turn further raises their risk of suicide (as well as of anxiety, depression, and other problems associated with suicidal behavior).

The research does not suggest that personal risk factors alone cause a child to be bullied. Rather, these personal characteristics act in conjunction with risk factors associated with two major aspects of a child's social life:

- The family, and its associated potential for child maltreatment, domestic violence, and parental depression.
- The school environment, including a lack of adequate adult supervision, a school climate characterized by conflict, a lack of consistent and effective discipline and even the enrollment size of the school.

A blog by Wayne Maines in the Huffington Post tells a moving story of parental love.

"I hugged her and said, 'some transgender kids do not have parents that love, accept and support them. Some parents may not have the resources or support needed to protect them. You have parents that love you very much, support you and are extremely proud of you. We will always be there for you. We will always protect you at home and at school.

That does not mean there are not people out there that might hurt you. You have to be very careful. You have to watch where you go, and whom you go with at all times. Never go anywhere alone.' "

It's a sad commentary that these children have to grow up in fear and with limits on their activity. But it's where we are as a society and bullies contribute to that fear.

The Gay, Lesbian & Straight Education Network (GLSEN), created the national "Day of Silence" on April 20, 2012 to remind people that anti-lesbian, gay, bisexual and transgender (LGBT) bullying, harassment and name-calling occurs every day in schools across the country. Measures like this are a beginning to help develop greater inclusiveness in America. But even closer to home, what you discuss with your children and the behaviors and level of tolerance you model become an essential part of improving the situation.

# Personality Will Impact How Your Child Responds to a Bullying Situation

Virtually every young person could be the victim of a bully. Bullying is at its core, a relationship. Relationships are probably the most important thing in life to kids growing up and forever after that. So as we try to be predictive of the risks our children are facing, we should know that researchers suggest that most of them adopt, consciously or not, one of three personality-based approaches as formulated by University of Illinois psychology professor Karen Rudolph, PhD.

## A focus on developing relationships

"Some are focused on developing their relationships. They want to improve their social skills. They want to learn how to make friends," she said.

Researchers found, as they expected, that children who were most interested in developing relationships "had more positive perceptions of themselves and were more likely to engage in proactive strategies to solve the problem," she said. This might involve asking a teacher for advice, or getting emotional support. Students with these goals also were less likely to engage in other impulsive responses to harassment, Dr. Rudolph said.

### A FOCUS ON DEMONSTRATING COMPETENCE

Or they may try to demonstrate their competence by avoiding negative judgments. "These are the kids who say, 'I'm not going to do anything that's going to draw negative attention, that's going to make me look like a loser, that's going to embarrass me,' " Dr. Rudolph said.

Children who wanted to be perceived as cool or competent "were less likely to use those kinds of thoughtful, careful strategies" when dealing with harassment, Dr. Rudolph said. "And they were more likely to retaliate." These children also had more negative perceptions of their peers, Dr. Rudolph said.

### A FOCUS ON AVOIDING NEGATIVE JUDGMENTS

Children who wanted to avoid negative judgments were less likely to retaliate against their peers. "But they were also more passive. They just ignored what happened," she said. This approach might be useful in some circumstances, especially for boys who tend to be more physically aggressive and more likely to retaliate than girls, Rudolph notes. But passive responses also may increase a bully's willingness to "up the ante," she said

In the study Dr. Rudolph noted that the objective was to better understand children's social goals in harassment situations in order to lead to better interventions. "Focusing on the goals that kids develop in their social relationships is important to understanding their actions," she summarized.

# Brothers and Sisters Will Have Conflict, Constantly, Minimize the Chaos By Not Buying Into the Provoking Behaviors

As we prepared this book, we passed long evenings sharing many common experiences as parents.

Like it or not, families are evolving social systems and there is a "pecking order" that is generally in place. The dominance-seeking child will often anger everyone in an effort to demand attention — even if that attention is negative. This can be the younger child or the older child, as dominance isn't always a function of birth order.

There are times when it feels anything but, sibling conflict is fairly normal. But while it may always be part of family life it becomes especially troubling when one child uses physical force or dominance to come out ahead.

The commentary of Dr. Lisa Damour on a very enlightening radio program we heard on an April 2012 "Civic Commons" PBS program in Ohio gave us some valuable insight.

Dr. Damour notes that research has found that among children in the same family in the same space, there are an average of sixty conflicts per hour!

**"Expose the provoking behavior."**

Dr. Damour had a good suggestion that she says generally helps the situation: call out the provocation itself.

Each of the siblings knows exactly how to initiate a confrontation with the other. And they use it at will, she notes. What she suggests as an effective strategy is simply not to accept either child's version of what happened, but rather to expose the provoking behavior and identify its source.

She explains that the parent has an option of shifting the blame to the provoking child, to cut off the conflict at its inception.

# Carefully Observe Your Child's Friends

**Make your home welcoming** to your child's friends. This is the best way to monitor these young people and observe their interaction.

Ask your child about these friends — where they live, what they like to do. If possible, get to know the parents or guardians.

With younger children, be skeptical if they don't seem to have a firm curfew or a supportive older family member available to drop them off or pick up them up.

Involving your child in sports or music helps open the door to get to know the parents of kids who make up at least part of your child's circle. You have a lot of time in the stands or in rehearsals with these folks.

And you can set your watch by these youngsters hanging out both on and off the field.

Peer influence weighs heavily on all children. It's important to know who is helping to shape your child.

# Early Warnings

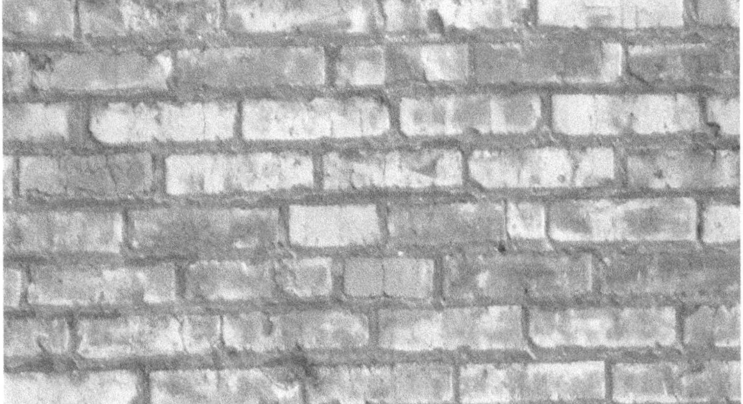

# Be Skeptical of Teasing

It's fairly safe to say that just about every one of us has been on both ends of teasing.

Most conventional wisdom tells us that when teasing comes in the form of playful banter, it doesn't have much potential for harm.

There's also not much evidence that the more benign and playful forms of teasing, the kind that touches upon another's sensitivity but doesn't really stay too long, is a direct "gateway drug" for bullying.

And it doesn't mean that teasing can't result in temporary or even lasting emotional harm, particularly if it's directed to someone's appearance. Teenagers in particular are already self-conscious about their physical appearance and highly sensitive to the typical adolescent body transformations. So the kind of intrusive and ongoing teasing that can come from parents, siblings and peers can cross the line to bullying. And sometimes, it may be a fine line.

Some clarity and points of distinction between teasing and bullying, including the different effects on boys and girls, is provided by Dr. Nancy

Darling with some helpful insights in Psychology Today in a 2010 article "Teasing and Bullying, Boys and Girls."

Dr. Darling notes that "unlike bullying, victims help determine the meaning of teasing" which she further defines as "an ambiguous social exchange that can be friendly, neutral, or negative."

We would insist that many children mask their emotions, pretending to be amused, and then run home and cry in their pillow.

With bullying, including verbal harassment or aggression, the intent is generally to hurt the victim, and the victim's reaction doesn't determine the meaning of the bully's action. It is overtly hostile and almost nothing the victim does will change that.

Classic observational research by developmental psychologist Ritch Savin-Williams and by Donna Eder suggests that teasing tends to work differently for adolescent boys and girls. Among boys, teasing tends to establish a fairly strict and stable hierarchy — who's on top, who gets listened to, who makes decisions. Teasing includes small insults, physical bumps and pushes, and minor insults.

**"The ability of boys to exchange insults and tease each other with no one getting angry is a critical sign that boys are real friends."**

Dr. Darling adds to that contention with her research-based observation that the ability of boys to exchange insults and tease each other with no one getting angry is a critical sign that boys are real friends.

Dr. Darling's article also notes that it doesn't work that way for girls. Girls' status hierarchies are much more unstable than boys'. By teasing, slights, and petty remarks, girls' hierarchies are "set by asking favors — high status girls impose on lower status ones — and giving compliments — low status girls compliment higher status ones."

Girls' aggression is typically less physical and subtler than the aggression of boys.

It is sometimes difficult to know if your child is exaggerating harmless teasing. Nevertheless, it is not fair to expect young people to be fully equipped to deal with ridicule of any kind, no matter the intent.

Most experts agree that bullying has the following characteristics:

Bullying is repeated (frequent) intentional actions that bring harm.

Bullying involves an imbalance of power between the bully and victim.

Bullying is a relationship in which one individual seeks to gain power and control over the life of another.

To find out more about the differences between bullying and teasing, take EduGuide's quiz "Is this Teasing or Bullying?" by visiting http://www.eduguide.org/.

# Watch for Warning Signs of Today's Bully

While the bully can have many faces, there are two types of widely divergent kids who seem more likely than others to engage in bullying behaviors:

The first are well connected to their peers, have social power, are overly concerned about their image and like to dominate or be in charge of others.

The other group tends to be isolated from their peers and may be depressed or anxious, have low self-esteem, be less involved in school, be easily pressured by peers and not identify with the emotions or feelings of others.

In addition to those major areas, some other traits supportive of bullying behavior are found in children who:

- Are aggressive or easily frustrated
- Have less parental involvement or are having issues at home
- Think badly of others

- Have difficulty following rules
- View violence in a positive way
- Have friends who bully others

Remember, bullies are not always physically stronger or bigger than those they bully. The power imbalance can come from a number of sources including popularity and high cognitive ability — and children who bully may even have both of these otherwise positive attributes.

# Is Your Child Becoming a Bully? Be Alert to These Indicators

If you ask your child if he or she is bullying someone you can guess what the answer will be. That's why as parents, we have to be watchful and intuitive. And fortunately there are some clues.

### Here are some indicators that your child is becoming a bully.

- Highly competitive and obsessed with winning, effective for an athlete but it can get out of control
- Associates with young people who are constantly in trouble or act disrespectfully to others in the neighborhood
- Exhibits overly controlling behavior at home, probably happening at school as well
- Uses put downs and derogatory names in everyday language and/or online

- Has been bullied in the recent past as bullied children can become bullies
- Takes offense when being asked to comply with a request
- Shows a growing disrespect for others and never sympathizes with those less fortunate — a lack of empathy is developing
- Is surrounded by followers, usually a group of children who look to your child as a role model

**"If a child suddenly stops talking to his or her best friend, that friend may be the bully."**

- Academics are suffering, grades slumping
- His or her school counselor voicing concerns

As children grow, their friends and activities do change, but usually not the basic ones. If a child suddenly stops talking to his or her best friend, that friend may be the bully.

If your child suddenly gives up on an activity or a hobby they used to love, the bully might also be involved in that activity.

Children, especially teenagers, go through emotional extremes. There is, however, a big difference between a mood swing and a change in character, a common sign of bullying.

# Your Reaction To Bullying

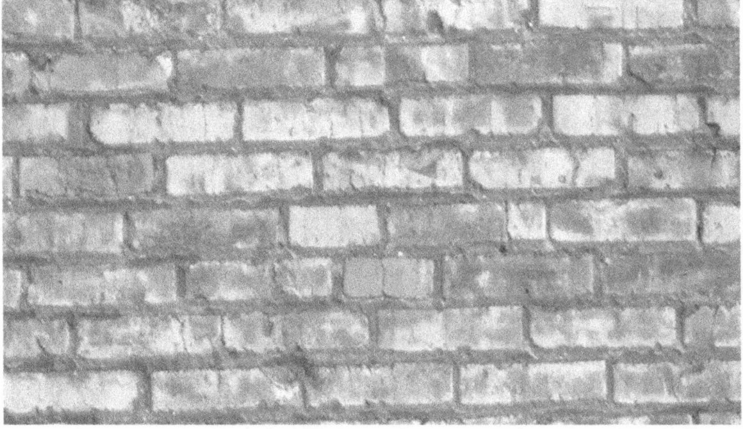

# Important Do's and Don'ts

THE BEST WAY TO send the message that bullying behavior won't be tolerated is to respond to it quickly and consistently. Keep in mind these immediate steps you should take, or avoid, to help keep your child and other children safe:

## Do,

- Intervene immediately. And don't hesitate to get help from another adult.
- Separate the kids involved.
- Make sure everyone is safe.
- Meet any immediate medical needs.
- Stay calm. Reassure the kids involved, including bystanders.
- Model respectful behavior when you intervene.

### Don't:

- Ignore it and think the kids can work it out without adult help.
- Immediately try to sort out the facts.
- Force other kids to say publicly what they saw.
- Question the children involved in front of other kids.
- Talk to the kids involved together, only separately.
- Make the kids involved apologize or patch up relations on the spot.

### Get police help or medical attention right away if:

- A weapon is involved.
- There are threats of serious physical injury.
- There are threats of hate-motivated violence, such as racism or homophobia.
- There is serious bodily harm.
- There is sexual abuse.
- Anyone is accused of an illegal act, such as robbery or extortion—using force to get money, property, or services.

# It Is a Crime To Assault Another Person, It Is Also a Civil Case.

If drilling down a little further reveals that bullying has, in fact, been taking place consider that in this nation, it is a crime to assault another person. And you don't have to actually touch someone else to be charged with assault. A feigned punch or threatening gesture can be classified as assault.

People that carry out these acts can face a judge.

In fact, in addition to being a criminal act for which one may be charged and tried, assault is also a civil offense for which the person being assaulted may sue for damages, including mental distress. Lawsuits are also being directed toward alleged damages suffered through social media. Attempted character assassination, often the cyberbully's primary tool, can be very costly.

# The Four Things You Should Never Do

- Never tell the child to ignore the bullying.
- Do not blame the child for being bullied. Even if you suspect some provocation, retaliation in the form of bullying is unacceptable. No one deserves to be bullied.
- Do not tell the child to physically fight back against the bully. That kind of advice could lead to injury as well as suspension or expulsion from school.
- Resist the urge to contact the other parents involved. It may make matters worse. School or other officials can act as mediators between parents.

# Kids Can Be Slow to Reveal Being Bullied, Signs to Watch for

**Bullies attempt to humiliate,** intimidate, or harm a person seen as weaker or different. Be watchful. Most kids who are bullied are slow to reveal what they are experiencing. Instead, there may be an unexpected drop in grades or your child may have a pessimistic sense atypical of his or her normal outlook.

You may notice the child shies away from eye contact, and may be reluctant to get up and go to school. Perhaps there is trouble with sleeping.

One of more of these clues may emerge if your child is experiencing bullying.

Older teenagers may seem to withdraw from the family and spend less time with parents and siblings. Another caution light appears if they become verbally profane and develop an angry demeanor.

With younger kids, the situation is basically reversed, and your radar should light up if the child doesn't want to leave your sight. Sometimes this clinginess may be part of other issues related to security, but it can also be a sign of a stronger fear.

The Permanente Medical Group's *My Doctor Online* offers symptomatic clues such as a child complaining of frequent headaches or stomach aches. The physicians also alert parents to a change in eating habits or even the age-old stolen lunch money, which results in a very hungry child after school.

They may have trouble sleeping and report experiencing bad dreams.

They may begin to "lose" personal possessions.

They may attempt to avoid school.

### "Is everybody treating you okay?"

They may be noticeably anxious leaving home for school.

Fewer friends visit the home.

There are unexplained injuries or damaged clothing or school items.

Older children may skip school to avoid contact with the bully.

"They may become moody, anxious, sad, or withdrawn. Some victims of bullying begin to hurt themselves, such as by cutting on themselves. Victims of bullying often feel helpless or develop low self-esteem, blaming themselves for the bullying or feeling like they are not good enough to belong in a social setting."

One very effective question to ask a child who you may suspect is being bullied is "Is everybody treating you okay?" It's an inquiry that can open the door for children who may be having difficulty expressing their concern. If the answer is "not really…" then explore that response privately and deeply.

# The Five Kinds of Bullying Today

### Threats

The intimidation involved in simple name-calling does not seem to have sufficient impact today for bullies, so they move beyond that point to specific threats against the safety of others.

### Profanity

The issue of public profanity directed to another person, and an overall lack of civility is an important component of the bullying issue in our society. The bully's communications often escalate from name-calling to overall profane statements intended to both threaten and diminish the self-esteem of the victims.

### Cyber Attacks

Some young people in America today have graduated from one-on-one interaction to the ability to commit computer-based attacks against multiple people. Today's Bully has at his or her disposal an arsenal of interactive ways to attack many individuals without remorse at the touch of a button.

### Hazing

To understand the impact of hazing on our society, it's important to view it as a continuum that often starts long before the traditional college fraternity hazing or even the kind of hazing that despite increased scrutiny, exists in military training. Hazing occurs as early as elementary school where children are asked to join clubs and continues into youth sports, middle school and high school and on into college.

### Assault

Authorities in recent years have brushed off many social confrontations, labeling them "bullying incidents," even when assault and battery has occurred.

Fortunately, this is rapidly changing. The negligent reaction to physical force creates victimization and diminishes accountability. Never dismiss assault as bullying. Call it out for what it is.

# Be Alert for Signs of Self-Harm Risk in a Bullied Child

*The number one goal* of almost every teenager is to be accepted by his or her peers.

If things get off track, the daily anxiety and stress can lead to a demoralized and depressed state.

Parents have to stay fully aware for warning signs. Our kids may not want us to know about their troubles; so becoming an investigator for your kid's sake is paramount.

The Permanente Medical Group provides this important message about the affects of bullying:

"For the victim of bullying, long-term consequences can range from feeling tense, afraid, depressed, or anxious to more severe physical and psychological results. Some children believe the only way to remove themselves from bullying is to avoid school and social settings or to take more drastic measures, such as responding with violence or even inflicting self-harm."

**"For every suicide among young people, there are at least 100 suicide attempts."**

Not only is Today's Bully deploying new technology and carrying new weapons, but recent research indicates that its consequences can be tragic.

Suicide is the third leading cause of death among young people, resulting in about 4,400 deaths per year, according to the CDC. For every suicide among young people, there are at least 100 suicide attempts.

Bully victims are between 2 to 9 times more likely to consider suicide than non-victims, according to studies by Yale University.

## Frightening Statistics

A recent Center for Disease Control national survey revealed that in the 12 months preceding the survey:

Almost 13.8 percent of high school students had seriously considered attempting suicide.

10.9 percent of high school students had made a plan for how they would attempt suicide.

6.3 percent of high school students had attempted suicide one or more times.

The Suicide Prevention Resource Center publishes guidance for educators and mental health professionals.

## Signs that a Young Person May Be at Risk for Suicide

- **A sudden deterioration in academic performance**

  Teens who were typically conscientious about their school work and who are now neglecting assignments, cutting classes, or missing school may be experiencing problems that can affect their academic success, behavior, and health and put them at risk of suicide.

- **Self-mutilation**
  Some young people resort to cutting their arms or legs with razor blades and other sharp objects to cope with emotional pain. Self-mutilation of this type is an unmistakable sign that something is wrong.
- **A fixation with death or violence**
  Teens may express this fixation in several ways:
  - ◊ **Poetry, essays, doodling, or other artwork**
  - ◊ **An obsession with violent movies, video games, and music**
  - ◊ **A fascination with weapons**
- **Unhealthy peer relationships**
  Teens whose circle of friends dramatically changes for no apparent reason, who don't have friends, or who begin associating with other young people known for substance abuse or other risk behaviors may be signaling a change in their emotional lives. Their destructive behaviors may discourage more stable friends from associating with them, or they themselves may reject former friends who "don't understand them anymore."
- **Volatile mood swings or a sudden change in personality**
  Students who become sullen, silent, and withdrawn, or angry and acting out, may have problems that have been associated with self-harm.
- **Indications that the student is in an unhealthy, destructive, or abusive relationship**
  This can include abusive relationships with peers or family members. Signs of a physically abusive relationship include unexplained bruises, swelling around the face or other, less noticeable injuries, particularly if the student refuses to discuss them.
- **Risk-taking behaviors**
  Risk-taking behaviors can be symptomatic of underlying emotional or social problems, especially when done by young

people who formerly did not engage in these activities. Such behaviors include:

- ◊ Unprotected or promiscuous sex
- ◊ Alcohol or other drug use
- ◊ Reckless driving, with or without a license
- ◊ Petty theft or vandalism

- **Signs of an eating disorder**

  Because of the related health risks, an eating disorder is an unmistakable sign that a child needs help. A dramatic change in weight that is not associated with a medically supervised diet may also indicate that something is wrong.
- **Difficulty in adjusting to gender identity**

  Gay, lesbian, bisexual, and transgender teens have higher suicide attempt rates than their heterosexual peers. While coming to terms with gender identity can be challenging for many young people, gay and lesbian youth face social pressures that can make this adjustment especially difficult.
- **Depression**

  Although most people who are clinically depressed do not attempt suicide, depression significantly increases the risk of suicide or suicide attempts. Symptoms of depression include the following:

### Be concerned if you observe:

- Sudden worsening in academic performance
- Withdrawal from friends and extracurricular activities
- Expressions of sadness and hopelessness, or anger and rage
- Sudden decline in enthusiasm and energy
- Overreaction to criticism
- Lowered self-esteem or feelings of guilt
- Indecision, lack of concentration, and forgetfulness
- Restlessness and agitation
- Changes in eating or sleeping patterns

- Unprovoked episodes of crying
- Sudden neglect of appearance and hygiene
- Fatigue
- Abuse of alcohol or other drugs as young people try to "self-medicate" their emotional pain

These signs are especially critical if the individual has attempted suicide in the past or has a history of or a current problem with depression, alcohol, or post-traumatic stress disorder (PTSD).

**The National Suicide Prevention Lifeline is 1-800-273-TALK (8255).**

**In Canada, if you are in crisis now dial the local emergency telephone number (often 911) in your area, and ask for the local Crisis Centre**

# Social Media Threats

# New Digital Dangers That May Be Invisible to Parents

The Baltimore Sun published an article on cyberbullying by writer Yvonne Wenger dealing with her assessment of why kids are engaging in it.

Ms. Wenger reported that young people, especially those in middle school and ninth grade, seek acceptance in peer groups with rules that can be "cruel or arbitrary."

Researchers note that young people will try to reduce their own insecurity at the expense of others, they are impulsive and tend to think in extremes, Ms. Wenger reported.

"With a click of a mouse, a teen can send a hurtful message without having thought twice."

Shaheen Shariff, Ph.D. Associate Professor, McGill University and Affiliate Scholar, Center for Internet and Society, Stanford University Law School, is a prominent expert on cyberbullying.

Dr. Shariff notes that cyberbullying is not the fault of digital technologies — "it is rooted in attitudes of discrimination, ignorance and power that have always been present in society."

What makes the difference may be numbers: a chorus of voices, especially online, can change the conversation. The presence of silent digital bystanders is particularly poisonous — the victim is invisible, and one joking comment can quickly set off a competitive string of nasty insults.

Teenagers don't realize that sending a link or adding to the hits can contribute to bullying, says Shariff, whose research shows that the larger the number of "cyber-voyeurs," the longer the bullying persists, and the worse it gets.

In an interview with the Montreal Gazette, Shariff said most of the youngest children who use Facebook and cellular phones "aren't aware that when they spread rumours or send sexually explicit text messages to their friends, such acts could get them in trouble with the law — including crimes such as libel, defamation of character and distribution and possession of child pornography."

She founded an online resource for parents, children, teachers and policy-makers on cyberbullying as part of a wider research project into the subject, called definetheline.ca.

Her website acts as a resource, but it also is a research tool to gain insight on cyberbullying and other online crimes. The website has sections written, designed and targeted for every age group with a section especially for parents:

"As the boundaries of legal responsibility become increasingly blurred online, we want to bring balance to the issues by clarifying and defining the point at which your child's joking and teasing of peers and teachers on social media might cross the line to become criminal harassment; where gossip and spreading of rumours traverses the invisible

### Prepare Yourself and Your Child for Cyberbullying

- Don't respond to the message
- Save the evidence
- Print it out if you can
- Tell a trusted adult right away

boundaries to result in civil liability or cyber-libel; and where "sexting," a relatively recent form of flirting among teenagers, now crosses the line and is sometimes treated by police as "child pornography."

## Sexting

Many teenagers believe that if messaging is consensual, then it's all right. While the First Amendment guarantee of freedom of speech is one we all cherish, there are dangers that go beyond the classic caveat of yelling "fire" in a crowded theater. The electronic possession or sending of revealing pictures, for whatever reason, is not only wrong, it could be a violation of the law.

In his book, "Ignorance Is No Defense: A Teenager's Guide to Georgia Law," author Tom Morgan notes that in Georgia, sexting, even if its consensual, can mean that your teenager can be charged with possession of child pornography, resulting in being registered as a sex offender, which can halt plans to go to college and a whole lot more.

Coach your teenagers on this very serious issue and tell them to delete any sexting message they receive, quickly. Tell them in no uncertain terms that this is one act that definitely isn't worth the potential consequence.

## Universities Assist Facebook in Developing New Tool

At the time of publication, Facebook is in the process of rolling out its newest addition, which allows teens to report mean or threatening posts by clicking the button "this is a problem."

Facebook teamed up with Yale, Columbia and the University of California at Berkley to create the new monitoring tool.

Ohio's WTVN TV News reporter John Potter describes the system as "aimed at 13 to 15-year-olds — with 13 being the minimum age for a user on the site."

"Clicking the new button takes users through a questionnaire to rank their emotions and determine how serious the problem is. Users then get a list of suggestions on how to resolve the issue based on how serious the complaint is. Depending on the situation, users can be prompted to send pre-written messages to their aggressor or to get help from a friend or adult," the news item noted.

There are also links to professionals for those who may be feeling depressed or suicidal.

## If You Observe Any of These Events, Your Child May Be a Cyberbully Victim And Not Telling You

- A change in behavior with their computer, or cell phone – avoids using these in front of you or talking about them
- Appears stressed when receiving an e-mail, instant message, or text
- Withdraws from friends, or acts reluctant to attend school and social events
- Exhibits signs of low self-esteem including depression and/or fear
- Grades begin to decline
- Lack of eating or sleeping

# You Are Paying the Bill, Control Your Child's Social Media

Know the websites your child visits and monitor online activities. Essentially, the online monitoring should take a similar direction as real world vigilance. Ask where your kid is going, what he or she is doing, and who your child meets online.

Tell your child that as a responsible parent you may review online communications if you think there is reason for concern. Installing parental control filtering software or monitoring programs are one option for monitoring your child's online behavior, but do not rely solely on these tools … because there's always a chance that your kid is one step ahead of you.

Have a sense of what he or she does online and in texts. Learn about these sites. Try out the devices they use.

Ask to "friend" or "follow" your kid on social media sites. As an alternative, have a reliable adult other than a parent/guardian, someone you and your child mutually trust, to provide this service.

For an even more direct approach ask for passwords, but promise you'll only use them in case of emergency. With this kind of request, make sure you convey the fact that you encourage and support their privacy and this isn't about removing that privacy completely, but rather that your concerns are strictly related to their safety and security.

And don't break your promise to respect their privacy solely because you're curious. The thing is, that fragile boundary between legitimate concern and snooping is easily crossed. A cautionary note: if you do choose to invade your child's privacy for something other than their safety and granted, as a parent or guardian you're pretty much the arbiter of what their safety entails, use your power very judiciously.

At the end of the day, that trust and the relationship you maintain, particularly through those often-tumultuous teenage years, is the most effective resource you have when it comes to influencing behavior.

**"Parents are blind to their kids' clandestine tactics."**

Encourage your child to tell you immediately if he or she is aware of anyone being cyber-bullied.

This dialogue requires the understanding that they won't be punished, particularly by taking away cell phones or online privileges, if they confide in you about a problem they are having or observing.

Bullying often takes place in areas hidden from adult supervision. Cyberspace has expanded that area considerably and bullies don't keep regular hours, so it goes on 24 hours a day. School officials are often powerless to stop it. Because no one's activities can be monitored constantly, there's always going to be a blind spot in the parental mirror, too.

You don't have to eliminate social media involvement. That would be both frustrating and futile. Just be keenly aware that the rapid expansion of social media is all encompassing. And like many things in life, it has its upside and its downside. For example, most kids have a cell phone which serves as a wonderful invention for keeping track of them and enhancing their safety. But the same cell phone can also be a formidable weapon in the hands of a bully.

What's clear about this new virtual world is that it not only complements traditional face-to-face communications, but replaces them in many instances. Twitter, YouTube, Facebook, Tumblr, Pininterest, Foursquare, and whatever else will be out there by the time you read this are close at hand for most children today. And that level of connectivity pales in comparison to texting.

The July $6^{th}$, 2012 issue of Newsweek reports that the average teen "processes an astounding 3,700 texts a month …" more than double the figure estimated five years earlier. So what can you do in the face of this digital tsunami? Well, to begin you might have to adopt the old "if you can't beat them join them" philosophy, at least to be more familiar with the environment.

If you aren't using this technology yourself do the homework and understand the various platforms. Find out what each of them can do and why people — and more specifically, your children — are using them.

It's likely that you pay for your child's cell phone and online connectivity. So you have a right and a responsibility to monitor it for safety reasons.

You can also read the Facebook of your child's online "Friends." This simple act can reveal a lot of information about the kids and the content your child is exposed to on social media.

How many friends are in the group? Are they local? What information limits are set for various categories of friends? Facebook has three levels of security: Friends, Friends of Friends and Everyone.

What are your child's passwords to private content?

Young people don't like this. And that's an understatement. But they need to know you are watching.

Facebook provides suggestions for these settings and it's a good idea to sit down with your child to ensure these settings are correct.

You can also block specific people from viewing your profile. The Facebook site (Facebook Press Room, 2010) offers the following information for dealing with harassment:

"Cyberbullies often seek a reaction from the people they harass. When they fail to get one, they often give up gradually."

Rather than responding to a bully via Inbox, a Wall post, or Facebook Chat, you can use the *Block* or Report or *This is a problem* functions to resolve the issue safely.

Remember, only confirmed Friends can post to your child's Wall or send a message through Chat. If your child is receiving posts and Chat messages you don't like, you should consider insisting on removing the sender from the Friends list.

This is the first line of defense if another kid begins name-calling or other potentially bullying behavior. They cannot communicate with you when deletion renders the activity mute. Many potential escalating situations are stopped before they get out of hand by this one move. This is the only kind of bullying that has a chance to be stopped by ignoring it and shutting out the offender.

The simple action can be further strengthened if your kid's real "friends" also delete the bullying child from their Friends list.

Please note that you should also contact the authorities if your child ever feels threatened by something you see on the site. Many school systems are now mandated to become involved if their students are cyber bullied by another student. A growing number of schools are mandated to have a protocol in place for helping cyberbullied children.

Also, be aware that your child may put up another Facebook page under a different name if they really want to game the system. Careful observation may reveal this secret site. But most likely, you will need to have a truthful conversation with your child, and convince him or her to remove it if it exists.

And again, as mentioned earlier, cell phone texts are a potent and even more widely used form of communication. A text can be instantly deleted.

Clever kids will rely on this potential as a work around for communications they don't want you to see.

Your online telephone bill will reveal the telephone number and when texts are made by time of day and date. If your child is texting at 2:00 am, there's an issue you need to deal with even if it's as relatively innocent as lack of sleep. If your kid is texting dozens of times a day to a number, ask whose number that is.

# When Cyberbullying Becomes a Crime

**When cyberbullying involves the** following activities it is considered a crime and should be reported to law enforcement:

- Threats of violence
- Child pornography or sending sexually explicit messages or photos
- Taking a photo or video of someone in a place where he or she would expect privacy
- Stalking and hate crimes

Some states are developing laws that consider overt forms of cyberbullying itself criminal even when it doesn't include existing statutes.

Legislation signed by New York Governor Andrew Cuomo in July 2012 requires New York schools to establish protocols to not only deal with bullying, but also online harassment beginning in 2013.

The legislation defines bullying, harassment and discrimination as including, but not limited to, acts based on a person's actual or perceived race, color, weight, origin, ethnic group, religion, religious practice, disability, sexual orientation, gender or sex.

Legal protection against cyberbullying isn't universal at this point, but it's definitely trending. Be sure to consult your state's laws as well as local law enforcement agencies for specific guidance.

# The Bullying Child

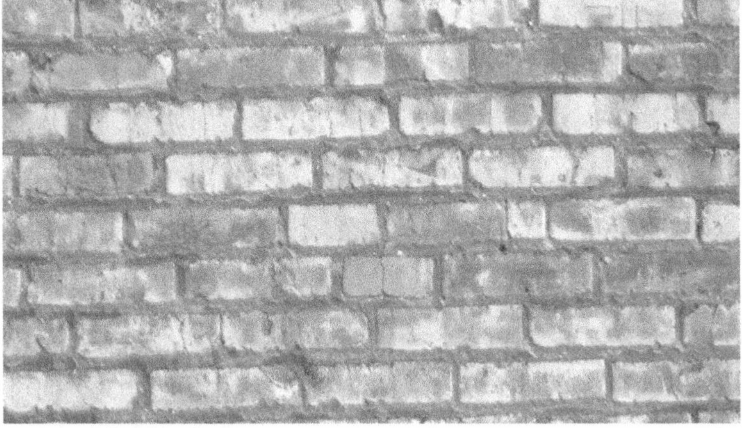

# Physical Bullying is a Boys' World

**Boys heed the call** of the culture. Niceness doesn't sell. The Eagle Scout is not loudly applauded in peer groups. The hip-hop artist is king, or the domineering athlete. Acceptance is the desired outcome of all behaviors.

Our National Center for the Prevention of Community Violence and Christopher Newport University hosted "Bullying Prevention: Community Solutions to a Community Problem" in March of 2012.

This daylong conference for educators, youth service providers, parents and community stakeholders focused on solutions to bullying that can be implemented in the classroom, at home and throughout the community.

Dr. Jackson Katz keynoted the event. Dr. Katz is internationally recognized for his groundbreaking work in educating students about gender violence prevention in relation to bullying, the sports culture and the military, as well as for his pioneering work in critical media literacy.

Keynoting the event, he offered that, for the most part, bullying is done by boys. The statistics that support this assertion are compelling and for some fairly clear reasons.

"We are raising generations of boys in a society that in many ways glorifies sexually aggressive masculinity and considers as normal the degradation and objectification of women," Dr. Katz told the Los Angeles Times in an interview prior to the conference.

"Consider: Misogynistic music and videos, the sexual bullying by entertainers such as Howard Stern, the growing presence of pornography and female stripping in mainstream culture and the crude displays of male dominance in professional sports."

Dr. Katz' presentation at the Christopher Newport University Bullying Conference included a visual review of the male stereotype in our society.

He examined current male imaging in music, movies, and sports and compared it to past examples, demonstrating how we've upped the ante over time. We now provide role models that are unreachable for most young men. So they compensate with weapons and brutality.

**"Gender is a vital factor, perhaps the vital factor."**

"When the perpetrators are boys, our media talk in a gender-neutral way about kids or children, and few delve into the forces—be they cultural, historical, or institutional—that produce hundreds of thousands of physically abusive and violent boys every year. Instead, we call upon the same tired specialists who harp about the easy accessibility of guns, the lack of parental supervision, the culture of peer-group exclusion and teasing, or the prevalence of media violence."

"All of these factors are of course relevant, but if they were the primary answers, then why are girls, who live in the same environment, not responding in the same way? The fact that violence—whether of the spectacular kind represented in the school shootings or the more routine murder, assault, and rape—is an overwhelmingly male phenomenon should indicate to us that gender is a vital factor, perhaps the vital factor," Dr. Katz says.

**"The issue is not just violence in the media but the construction of violent masculinity as a cultural norm."**

He notes that looking at violence as gender-neutral has the effect of blinding us as we desperately search for clues about how to respond.

"The issue is not just violence in the media but the construction of violent masculinity as a cultural norm. From rap music and videos, Hollywood action films and professional and college sports, the culture produces a stream of images of violent, abusive men and promotes characteristics such as dominance, power and control as means of establishing or maintaining manhood."

Dr. Katz asks us to consider, for example, professional wrestling, with its mixing of sports and entertainment and its glamorization of the culture of dominance. It represents, in a microcosm, the broader cultural environment in which boys mature. Some of the core values of the wrestling subculture—dominant displays of power and control, ridicule of lesser opponents, respect equated with physical fear and deference—were factors in the social system of Columbine High, where the shooters were ridiculed, marginalized, harassed, and bullied.

These same values infuse the Hollywood action-adventure genre that is so popular with boys and young men. In numerous films starring iconic hyper-masculine figures like Arnold Schwarzenegger, Sylvester Stallone, Wesley Snipes, and Mel Gibson, the cartoonish story lines convey the message that masculine power is embodied in muscle, firepower, and physical authority.

Dr. Katz's keen observations are echoed by the insights of Jessie Klein in her book "THE BULLY SOCIETY—School Shootings and the Crisis of Bullying in America's Schools."

"Instead of the range of emotions (marginally) available to girls," Klein writes, "boys are permitted to feel only anger and are encouraged to control their other feelings," to present a mask of masculinity.

Klein's observation that boys feel pressured to display "flamboyant heterosexuality."

In today's schools, kids bullying kids is an everyday reality where children learn early that being sensitive, respectful, and kindness earn them little respect.

# Girl Bullies Use Different Weapons

When that far smaller number of girls does turn to bullying, some of the more common characteristics to look for are jealousy, feelings of superiority, poor impulse control, and lack of empathy.

Leading researcher on the subject, Dr. Charisse Nixon, believes girls engage in bullying behavior when their basic needs of acceptance (by self), belonging (among others), control, and meaningful existence—are thwarted.

Dr. Nixon calls these needs the "ABCs, and me."

"They've learned the habit of bullying at home. Bullies often (but not always) come from homes where they are bullied or abused by their parents or older siblings. Bullying is a way for them to regain some of the control they have lost at home."

Dr. Nixon believes them to be insecure. In many cases, she says, bullying is a cover-up for insecurity. A bully may be sensitive about her weight or clothes, and bullying other girls allows her to attack them before they attack her.

"They need to feel powerful. They often gang up on another girl to demonstrate their control. They want to get attention and be popular."

"They have personal issues. Quite often, a girl may bully because she is having troubles at home or at school, which cause her to act out against other girls. Underneath her tough exterior, she is likely to be angry or depressed about other issues in her life," Dr. Nixon states.

Although physical violence is growing more commonplace in girl bullying, the usual method of bullying is verbal, either directly to the victim or behind the victim's back, or social media character sabotage.

Girls also can use exclusion as a bullying tactic — deliberately leaving one girl out of "the crowd."

Girl bullies will make anonymous phone calls (more difficult to do these days but still possible), using scare tactics or direct threats. All of these ugly encounters are happening every day, everywhere.

## The High Price of Being a Bully

Susan Davis, the insightful writer for *WebMD Magazine* notes that the topic of girl bullying is not new.

"Dozens of lay books and scholarly journals have explored the ways relational aggression -- tactics such as exclusion, rumor mongering, and Internet harassment -- can damage girls' self-esteem," she observes.

**"These girls learn to manipulate people like chess pieces."**

But only recently have researchers begun looking at what bullying does to the bullies themselves. The news is not good.

Davis refers to the work of Dr. Nixon in helping us understand this problem.

"In the short term, girl bullies often are rejected by peers and lack meaningful relationships," notes Charisse Nixon, PhD, co-author of "Girl Wars: 12 Strategies That Will End Female Bullying" and an assistant professor of developmental psychology at Pennsylvania State University in Erie.

Over time, "these girls learn to manipulate people like chess pieces," Nixon says. "Unfortunately, this can harm their ability to have meaningful relationships and successful careers."

## What To Do if Your Daughter Is Accused of Being a Bully

First, whether a boy or a girl, an accusation needs to be proven.

Go on a fact-finding mission that hopefully will lead to the truth. Find out who is involved. If a group is involved be sure to get information from multiple people. Did your daughter react to what she thought was bullying? Once all the facts are in, and it's clear that there is some credibility to the accusation, confront her and express your feelings regarding her treatment of others. Let her know what your further expectations will be.

Initially, apologies are in order to the girl or girls who have been affected by her behavior. Acknowledging the mistake provides an emotional release that is helpful in repairing the damage — both to the child bullied and the bully herself.

If the bullying is being done within a social network, remove or provide greater control to its access.

**"Acknowledging that one has made a mistake is an emotional release."**

Many girls have a bumpy road in maturing, understanding conflict and navigating the hurdles of growing up. But bullying is a decision — a decision to initiate a conflict, bringing discomfort to others.

So the ultimate strategy should be to restore empathy and kindness in her behavior.

# If Your Child Becomes a Bully, New Ground Rules Are Essential

When you hear from others that your child is bullying others, don't think of it as an indictment of your parenting or some family dysfunction. Simply consider it to be a wake-up call and be glad you heard it.

**"Remember that the victims of bullying include the bully and the bystanders."**

Then its time for some action and the first step is for your child to apologize to the bullied child and his family.

After that, do a quick social audit on your child's social circle. There's a good chance that looking at who your kid is hanging around with will offer some clues related to influences.

Then establish new ground rules. Create opportunities to develop new interests and be around different young people. Do everything parentally possible to change the social pattern. The power of peer groups and networks is profound so even a small alteration in the circle could be helpful.

If restrictive punishment is imposed, enable the child to earn his or her way out by good behaviors.

Remember that the victims of bullying include the bully and the bystanders. Beyond any punishment at home, the bully will be paying a large price for this behavior.

The Permanente Medical Group offers this advice to us:

Use positive discipline. Remove privileges or use other means to discipline your child so they learn their bullying behavior is not acceptable. "Using physical discipline to punish your child for abusing another child is not helpful. In fact, it's counter productive. Explain to your child how his or her behavior hurt another child."

Work with school officials. Make a plan with the school counselor, teacher, and principal to help your child move away from harmful behavior.

It is possible for your child to replace bad behavior with good, but he or she will need your guidance.

# The Bullied Child

# Confronting the Parents

*The unfortunate truth is* that it's very likely that the bully your child encounters won't be a stranger. You may know the bully, too and there's a chance you may know the bully's family.

However, we would suggest confronting them only if you have a strong existing relationship.

If you are on good solid footing with the bully's family, approach them in a calm manner and let them know the facts, as you understand them, as well as the effect the behavior is having on your child. If you can, get those facts from the perspective of both kids. If you do not have that kind of relationship, it's best to go through the school or whatever other organization/authority may be involved.

**"You never know."**

If you do try a direct approach, be aware that talking about someone's child may even surpass discussions of money when it comes to unexpected reactions and previously unimagined behavior from people you know, or at least think you know. Not only may the parents not be cooperative, they may be downright defensive. Or worse, blame the victim.

If that's the case realize that the friendship may be at stake and just move on to letting the school authorities drive the resolution. After that resolution takes place the parents may remain in denial and the friendship will likely be altered, but you still have to do the right thing.

If you don't know the other family involved keep in mind that in today's public school environment, people from vastly different walks of life with considerably divergent values and life experiences have all brought their children together to be educated in the same space. Therefore, we urge parents to ask school officials to serve as the intermediary with both the child and the parents.

# Teach Your Child to Stand Firm

**Any confrontation brings anxiety** and the bully encounter is an especially vulnerable and sensitive time. Your child needs to know you stand with him or her and that you will intervene if necessary. But while your role has to be clearly defined, it's important that your child is also prepared to take a stand.

Kristie Pattison, a guidance counselor at the Marbletown Elementary School in Stone Ridge, New York suggests some specific verbal responses to an initial act of bullying in *Highlights.* Given Ms. Pattison's role in elementary education these suggestions would tend to be more effective with younger children.

"We try to give kids many examples of what to say if they're being bullied. Humor and assertiveness both work well.

"If someone is making fun of someone's appearance, a child can say, 'I like myself and my ears.' "

"When a bully is angry, kids need to learn to walk away and say, 'I'll talk to you when you've calmed down.' "

"Besides verbal strategies, body language is important. Kids need to learn to feel confident and look confident," she suggests.

We suggest that you teach your child how to "stand firm" in the physical sense, too: shoulder back, head up, eye contact with the bully. This kind of body language can help send a signal that the bully's attempt at intimidation isn't working. Bullies tend to single out those who are conveying a sense of vulnerability, so help your child avoid projecting it.

As an analogy, in youth baseball we taught our batters to approach the plate confidently, establish eye contact with the pitcher and take a big practice swing. This lets the pitcher know the kid at the plate means business. It also instills confidence in the hitter and hopefully, some doubt on the mound.

# Twelve Things to Consider When Your Child Has Been Bullied

- **Listen and focus on your child**. Learn what's been going on and show that you will help.
- **Assure your child that bullying is not their fault.** Some kids may harbor the notion that somehow, they must deserve this treatment and a sense of shame is present.

**"Reporting these actions to law enforcement is one counter-measure that should be on the table."**

- **Determine if what has occurred is a crime.**
  Too often we ignore the fact that a crime has occurred by labeling the incident as childhood bullying. Assault, vandalism and theft are crimes that may occur in bullying incidents. Reporting these actions to law enforcement is one counter-measure that should be on the table.

- **Do not tell your child that you will not inform or involve others.**
  Stopping the bullying will very likely mean that other adults will be informed and will, by necessity, get involved.
- **Know that kids who are bullied may struggle with talking about it.**
  Consider referring your child to a school counselor, psychologist, or other mental health service.
- **Give advice about what to do.**
  This may involve role-playing and thinking through how the child might react if the bullying occurs again.
- **Work together to resolve the situation and protect the bullied child.**
  The child, parents, and school or organization may all have valuable input. It may help to ask the child being bullied what can be done to make him or her feel safe.
- **Remember that changes to routine should be minimized and shared.**
  He or she is not at fault and should not be singled out. For example, consider rearranging classroom or bus seating plans for everyone. If bigger moves are necessary, such as switching classrooms or bus routes, the child who is bullied should not be the only one forced to change.
- **Develop a game plan.**
  Maintain open communication between schools, organizations, and parents. Discuss the steps that are taken and the limitations around what can be done based on policies and laws. Remember, the law does not allow school personnel to discuss discipline, consequences, or services given to other children.
- **Be persistent.**
  Commit to making it stop and insist on firm actions.

- **Encourage your child to hang around close, trusted friends.** Walk to and from school with supportive classmates.
- **Let your child's friends know what is going on.** Sharing the information gives them a chance to apply peer pressure to have it stopped. The social climate at the school can be changed to promote the message that bullying is unacceptable/ uncool and it is courageous to stand up individually or as a group for someone who is being bullied.

# Bullying of Any Kind Can Result in Lifelong Emotional Damage and Why Professional Counseling Should Be Considered

Researchers trying to get a clear understanding of the long-term effects of bullying and what they refer as "peer victimization" have asked adults to recount school-age bullying experiences.

Their findings are telling. Patricia McDougall, Shelley Hymel and Tracy Vaillancourt, PhD note that memories of childhood bullying and teasing are associated with high rates of depression, social anxiety, pathological perfectionism, and greater neuroticism in adulthood.

When you look at the content of how adults describe their childhood victimization experiences, according to research reports, it does appear that "over time many victims report a reduction in their hurt feelings (for example, less unhappiness, decreased shame)."

"Yet, for those who consider the bullying to have been extremely painful, the troubling feelings continue with reported long-term negative effects on both personality and attitudes. In short, childhood bullying is a highly memorable experience and recollections of these events show no evidence of forgetting."

**"Bullying sets the child off on a trajectory that impacts his or her entire life."**

Bullies also pay a heavy price.

Many of the individuals who considered themselves to be bullies have been self-characterized in later life as angry, depressed, aggressive and hostile. They tend to be domineering. They have a lot of conflict with friendships.

Bullying sets the child off on a trajectory that impacts his or her entire life. And it has the potential to impact the education, the career, the happiness and even the health of the bully in later years.

Dr. Dan Olweus is a pioneering researcher in the field of bullying prevention and the founder of the highly lauded Olweus Bullying Prevention Program. Years ago, he documented a connection between bullying and later criminal behavior.

Dr. Olweus' research showed that 60% of those who bullied in grades 6 and/or 9 had at least one criminal conviction by age 24; 35-40% had three or more convictions (as compared to a group of non-bullying boys).

Another research group in England asked boys about whether they were bullies at age 14, then 18, and then again at age 32. The findings showed that "about one in every five boys (18%) who saw himself as "a bit of a bully" at age 14 continued to report being a bully at age 32. These adult bullies at 32 years of age were highly aggressive (61%) and had been convicted of violence (20%).

A 2009 study in the United Kingdom surveyed 2,000 students and found that nearly two-thirds of the students had witnessed bullying, 20 percent admitted they had been a bully themselves, and 34 percent indicated being a victim of bullying. Witnesses were more likely to exhibit the same mental health issues as bullies and victims, such as depression and interpersonal sensitivity, and were more likely than victims to engage in substance abuse.

"Bullying impacts all of us, whether we're actively participating or simply witnessing a bullying event," said Gary Henschen, M.D., chief medical officer for behavioral health at Magellan.

"We have to be mindful that people who witness bullying might be hurting, too, or may have difficulty dealing with the emotions of what they have experienced. It's more important than ever that we establish rules of respect and tolerance within our communities and online. When bullying happens, we all lose."

We really shouldn't assume that even small bullying incidents are fully repaired and processed by our kids.

Obviously, in the most extreme cases, deep emotional harm can result. But baggage can be carried away even from what appears to be a fully resolved case of bullying as well.

# Do Children Grow Out of Bullying?

A FASCINATING ARTICLE BY Patricia McDougall, Shelley Hymel and Tracy Vaillancourt, has been published by the website resource Education.com entitled "What Happens Over Time To Those Who Bully And Those Who Are Victimized?"

"Counter to the notion that 'children grow out of bullying,' our working assumption is that at least some school bullies move through life continuing to use aggressive strategies in romantic relationships, in the workplace and in other areas of their lives."

"In the case of victims, we would argue that there may be different pathways that people follow. For example, we expect that under the most extreme circumstances of school bullying, some who are victimized never truly recover and continue to have difficult and troubled lives well after they finish (or leave) school."

McDougall, Hymel and Vaillancourt also note that how victims fare will depend on how they see themselves and how they make sense of what happened to them.

"Stated simply, people who do not see themselves as a victim may be better adjusted in adulthood," they note.

Once the initial bullying is resolved, evaluate the need for professional counseling for your child to help process and repair the damage.

Whether the child has been the bully, the victim or the bystander, a professional counselor will help process and repair the damage, before he or she incorporates this life experience into baggage they will carry forever.

Victims of cyberbullying are also at risk for depression. A 2010 study found that victims of cyberbullying had even higher levels of depression than victims of face-to-face bullying.

Beyond solid personal counseling is another modality that is making news in helping victims of bullying and abuse.

Licensed Professional Counselor Beth Bennett-Hill in Charlotte, N.C. is among other therapists who have had consistent successes using a treatment modality called EMDR.

Eye Movement Desensitization and Reprocessing (EMDR) is a common treatment for Post Traumatic Stress Syndrome.

Not only has it been shown to be effective for trauma, it also seems to be effective for other types of upsets that can leave an individual with dysfunctional thoughts, behaviors and negative beliefs about themselves and the world around them.

In addition, it provides encouraging results as a treatment for panic, anxiety, phobias, lack of motivation, inability to make a decision, and substance abuse.

"I have been in practice for almost thirty years and since becoming trained in EMDR. I am seeing miracles of transformation take place in my office daily. Clients who have come to me after twenty years of talk therapy are now getting well. My clients continue treatment because they are experiencing the rapid progress that this treatment achieves and are experiencing hope," Bennett-Hill says.

In EMDR, the client is asked to bring up the upsetting event and to identify emotionally upsetting feelings, thoughts, images and negative beliefs about themselves related to the event.

With these in mind, the clinician stimulates the right and left-brain alternately by either eye movement or by tapping alternately on the back of the client's hands. This causes the brain to recall the event and move the event from the reptilian part of the brain (flight, fight, or freeze) to the cortex where the rational/cognitive information can inform the memory thus changing the dysfunctional reactions previously present.

"Admittedly I am biased towards the use of EMDR. When you witness daily the transformation of people's lives it is difficult not to be," she says.

You can obtain more information at www.emdr.com or www.emdrinaction.com. Finding a good therapist is the key to successful outcomes.

# Get Involved and Monitor Your Child's School Environment

**Put a lot of kids** in one place, not really of their choosing for the most part, and there will be conflict. Of course, not all conflict can be characterized as bullying.

Most formal definitions of bullying make a distinction between bullying and physical fighting between peers.

**"Distinguish bullying from peer fights where both kids are on pretty equal footing."**

Deborah Kotz of the Boston Globe notes that nearly all states have laws in place that require schools to take action against bullies and set up specific definitions to distinguish bullying from peer fights where both kids may be on a more equal footing.

Kotz notes that in these definitions, bullying needs to be repetitive and from a consistent source like one child or a group of children; it also involves dominant children against those who don't have the ability to adequately defend themselves and is mean-spirited, intending to cause a victim emotional or physical distress.

In most school environments, protocols are in place when bullying is reported. Parents need to monitor the progress of the school response. Insist on immediate action.

Administrators and faculty are now prompted to be more watchful of kids who are different — kids who are obese, shorter than most kids, openly gay or transgender, flamboyant in dress or mannerism, have a speech impediment, are extremely thin or isolated from other children. If your child fits any of these descriptions, you should be extremely watchful.

# Understand What Your School Should Be Doing When Bullying Occurs

AT THE CONCLUSION OF this book, as an Appendix, is a sample Bullying Policy prepared by the National Center for the Prevention of Community Violence. A glance through this model statewide policy should help parents understand the processes that need to be in place to assure that bullying incidents are responded to quickly and thoroughly. You can view what typical state policymakers may expect of every school administration.

**"Some disciplinary actions don't seem to work."**

Zero tolerance or more liberal "three strikes, you're out" strategies don't seem to work. Suspending or expelling students who bully does not reduce bullying behavior, at least statistically. In fact, it may have a counter effect because students and teachers may be less likely to report and address bullying if suspension or expulsion are the only possible consequences.

Dr. Dewey Cornell's study at the University of Virginia, announced in April of 2012, found that careful assessment and measured action is a more effective response to school violence than a one-size-fits-all, zero-tolerance approach. The study was conducted in 40 elementary, middle and high schools in Newport News, VA.

Students in schools that used a strategy to evaluate the seriousness of school violence, instead of automatic expulsion, are more likely to receive more appropriate responses for their actions, such as behavioral health counseling or parent conferences, and less likely to receive long-term suspensions or transfers to other schools.

"Threat assessment allows school administrators to return to the philosophy that the punishment should fit the crime, and that the school's response to a student should be based on the seriousness of the threat, rather than a one-size-fits-all approach that you see with zero tolerance," Cornell said.

According to Cornell, severe acts of violence in school are relatively rare, but threats of violence are much more common and pose a serious problem for the nation's schools. The widely used practice of automatic suspension increases the risk for academic failure and does not seem to improve student behavior, Cornell said.

"Our research has shown that schools which rely the most on suspension have the highest dropout rates," he said. "We know that suspension has deleterious effects on students and is counterproductive to our goal of helping them complete their education."

Threat assessment can actually help identify underlying problems, such as bullying or conflicts in friendships and romantic relationships, Cornell said. In other cases, there are disputes with teachers, learning problems or other difficulties that need attention.

"Schools using threat assessment showed a 79 percent reduction in bullying infractions and a 52 percent reduction in long-term suspensions," Cornell said.

"Sometimes this kind of student behavior may point to stressful circumstances leading to emotional distress, anger and depression. As a result, one goal of threat assessment is to initiate appropriate mental health counseling services for the student."

As part of the study, it was also demonstrated that schools receiving staff training in threat assessment showed significant improvements in staff understanding of the risk of student violence as well as changes in their attitudes toward zero tolerance and the use of suspension.

The schools were then followed for one school year. During this time, 201 students were identified by school authorities as making a threat of violence.

But does keeping a troublesome student in school jeopardize others' safety?

"Certainly there are a small number of students who are more safely educated in an alternative setting," said Professor Cornell. "But there is no evidence to indicate that a policy of keeping most students in school impairs the safety of others. Schools that use zero tolerance are not safer schools. The guidelines permit short-term suspensions for safety purposes in clearly specified cases, but almost all students are able to return to school."

Cornell said these guidelines are now being used in more than 1,000 Virginia schools as well as schools across the U.S. and in several other countries.

This evidence-based approach to bullying in the schools is particularly important because studies and experience show that traditional conflict resolution and peer mediation don't appear to be well suited to bullying. Bullying is not a conflict between people of equal standing who share equal blame. Facing those who have bullied may further upset kids who have been bullied.

Group treatment for students who bully is another strategy that hasn't had much success. The reason is that group members tend to reinforce bullying behavior in each other.

Our best advice for parents worried about a bullying environment is to know the school's leadership, make your own observations and ask a lot of questions.

Are the playgrounds and sports fields always properly monitored and supervised?

What about discipline and monitoring on the school bus?

Does your child's school have a bullying hotline that is promoted where every child can see it every day?

Is there a daily anti-bullying message communicated to the students?

Do the kids get involved in special events and observances to stop bullying?

Does your school's PTA support anti-bullying messages and measure and does it help parents understand the risks and dangers?

Is there an anti-bullying survey?

In Virginia in 2012, the Albemarle and Charlottesville school systems teamed up with The University of Virginia to identify bullying victims in every elementary, middle and high school in the Albemarle and Charlottesville districts

The Safe Schools/Healthy Students Albemarle/Charlottesville Project conducted a Peer Support Survey developed by the Curry School of Education (part of the University of Virginia).

**"Students more than anyone else know who is being bullied at school."**

The survey allows students and bullying victims to speak out anonymously. It also helps them understand the importance of coming forward and assists them in overcoming any embarrassment they may have. "Students more than anyone else know who is being bullied at school," said Professor Cornell.

Are gang members allowed to wear gang colors to your child's school?

Does the school system task a teacher or administrator to be anti-bullying supervisors in each school?

Has the school developed recording-keeping systems for bullying incidences?

How frequently has training taken place for the entire staff?

What measures have been taken for parent and community education about the steps taken by the district to eliminate bullying?

Especially in elementary schools, are there role-playing exercises so kids can rehearse their reactions to bullying situations?

What does your child, and his or her friends, think about the school security guards or assigned police officers?

The Office of Juvenile Justice and Delinquency programs of the Justice Department produces an excellent newsletter led by Administrator Jeff Slowikowski.

In the December 2011 edition, Slowikowski reviewed the Swedish National Council for Crime Prevention's recently issued recommendation for American schools.

In the report, "Effectiveness of Programmes to Reduce School Bullying: A Systematic Review," the authors make recommendations for anti-bullying programs in the United States.

These recommendations are based on their findings and an extensive literature review:

- Increase student engagement. Bullied children who remain engaged in school attend class more frequently and achieve more.
- Model caring behavior for students.
- Offer mentoring programs.
- Provide students with opportunities for service learning as a means of improving school engagement.
- Address the difficult transition between elementary and middle school (from a single classroom teacher to teams of teachers with periods and class changes in a large school.

- Start prevention programs early.
- Resist the temptation to use prefabricated curriculums that are not aligned to local conditions.
- Challenging academics, extracurricular activities, understanding teachers and coaches, and a focus on the future help keep victimized children engaged in their education.
- Schools, administrations, and districts that wish to stave off the negative effects of bullying must redouble their efforts to engage each student in school.

The interview data also highlighted what bullying victims need from their schools:

- A place of refuge where they can feel safe, appreciated, and challenged in a constructive way.
- Responsible adults who can support and sustain them and provide them examples of appropriate behavior.
- A sense of future possibility to persuade them that staying in school, despite the bullying, promises better things to come.

These factors allow bullied students to overcome the effects of bullying.

In contrast, the study participants agreed that superficial anti-bullying programs, grafted onto existing curriculums to fulfill a school district's responsibility to address bullying concerns, are an ineffective way to combat bullying.

## More of What Parents Can Do

There are basic and relatively easy ways that parents and caregivers can keep up-to-date with what's going on in school:

- Read class newsletters and school flyers and talk about them at home.

- Check the school website.
- Go to school events.
- Greet the bus driver.
- Meet teachers and counselors at "Back to School" night or reach out by email.
- Share phone numbers with other kids' parents.

# Youth Sports

# Adult Bully Behavior Needs to Be Challenged

THE DAY BEFORE EASTER in 2012, the bright morning sky is alive with wind and dogwood and the fresh green scent of the new leaves emerging from Virginia's grey brown winter. A glaring sunshine greets the first day of little league.

Three hundred little leaguers, from age 5 to 12, many with colorful shirts untucked and shoelaces still untied, gather at the Moose Lodge #25 field in a modest middle class subdivision of Newport News, Virginia.

The Moose Cal Ripkin Baseball Program is having Opening Day.

The field is beautifully lined with white chalk. The infield dirt is carefully raked. Dozens of older men and women, the hierarchy of the Moose Lodge, dot the sidelines filled with parents from all walks of life. Younger siblings scamper about and the hot dog stand is making a brisk business.

A hurried local photographer, who brings along several people to keep track of names and money, takes team pictures.

One assistant makes sure the kids raise the brims of their hats enough for the camera to see their eyes. Some kids smile, some don't. All want to get on with this and play baseball. Several forgot their hats.

The teams march onto the field as announced by the League's play-by-play man, a twelve-year-old who one day wants to be a sports announcer. The coaches try to keep order as the teams line up on the baselines.

Our young announcer inserts a twenty-year-old cassette into the player and a crackled version of the Star Spangled Banner accompanies the flag being raised by the nervous local Boy Scout troop.

The featured guest speaker takes the crackling microphone.

The man with the microphone is a veteran Little League Coach, high school official, parent of three children and national authority on youth violence.

"I know all you kids want to get on the field and play ball. This will only take a minute."

"I am only going to give you three charges today," he begins.

"First — to you kids… you're here to have fun and play the greatest game in the world. Don't ever think you are bigger than this game. The Moose has been playing baseball on this field for 57 years. You may be good, but be good with humility."

"Next — for you parents…your job is to be here and support your child, every game. That's your job. Be here for your son or daughter. Be the cheerleader, not the critic. But be here."

The speaker is Bobby Kipper, a quarter century veteran of the local police department, a former director of the DARE program, architect of one of the most successful gang prevention programs in America and co-author of the best selling book ***"No COLORS, 100 Ways to Keep Gangs from Taking Away Our Communities***, and ***No BULLIES."***

"Finally for the coaches…"

"This is not about you. It is not about domination. It is not all about which coach is the best coach. It's about the kids. Every one of them. As they compete, these kids respond to praise, not yelling. We do not need teams of bullies destroying their opponents here. We need good sports, gentle voices and praise for all these kids. Thank you."

Bobby Kipper walked off the field to cheers and applause.

People want civility in community life.

Our kids are taking a journey through the physical and emotional process of growing up, trying on different traits, experimenting with behaviors and listening for that referee's whistle.

With a new social consciousness related to the dangers of bullying, it's time to blow the whistle not only on kids bullying kids, but on adults bullying kids as well as other adults.

One of the most prevalent examples of this unfortunate behavior is in the realm of youth sports. If you have the occasion to be a spectator or participant in these activities, there's a good chance you've heard the baseball or basketball coach screaming at the kids, seen bullying behavior between coaches competing for the win or observed a bigger kid making dominant physical contact on a smaller kid just to make the point.

Coaches can nurture bullying among their players by not blowing the whistle on it.

Reporter Sarah Harris of the U.K. Daily Mail notes that a survey of 1,250 children aged eight to 16 found that 51.1 percent admitted to being a "victim of mental intimidation on sports fields" within Great Britain.

Across all ages, 67 percent witnessed some form of verbal abuse and 55 percent had seen physical violence such as a "player being tripped up, pushed over or kicked, or being struck with equipment such as a bat or racquet."

Even at age 8, the percentage of children who have witnessed violence while playing sports at school was 43 percent, Ms. Harris notes.

Competitiveness can be taught and modeled without being a bully.

Athletic role models are on the news — an NFL team that offers a bounty to its players to hurt the opposing players; major league pitchers intentionally throwing toward the batter's head; deliberate elbows to the head in professional basketball; blindside body slams in hockey. The camera brings it all to us every day.

"Looks like he won't be getting up," the commentator says as the station cuts to a commercial break while the injured player is removed.

We have to remember that youth coaches are volunteers and most are trying to do a good job, but they may be unconsciously using bully coaching practices. A gentle word may be all that is needed to adjust the coaching style. If that fails to get through, blow the whistle at the organizational level.

# FOUR PROMISES

## *Make An Agreement With Your Kids*

Here is an agreement we suggest would be very helpful to make with your children.

As a result of three decades of serving in law enforcement, in halting youth violence and championing for a level playing field for all our children, we have developed four basic promises we suggest you share with your child.

# Four Special Promises By You And Your Child

## By You,

I will be talking with you about bullying a lot.

If you encounter a bully, I will stand with you.
You will not have to grow up in fear.

I will never blame you. There is no excuse for anyone bullying you. It would not be your fault.

I need to know and understand your social media to help protect you from its dangers.

Please turn page…

## By Your Child,

**I will let you know of any encounter with bullying.**

**I will try to stand firm when a bully tests me for weakness.**

**I will not fight back. I will not be afraid to walk away.**

**I will be open and honest with you about my social media world.**

______________________________________

Signature of child

______________________________________

Signature of parent or guardian

*APPENDIX*

# Expect the Best of Your Child's School —Here is a Sample of a Benchmark School Bullying Policy

So that you can be an informed parent, we include this Model Bullying Policy developed by the National Center for the Prevention of Community Violence.

By familiarizing yourself with such a statewide bullying policy, you can see how detailed a typical school's process must be and, generally speaking, what you can expect from the school when your child encounters bullying.

## Model Policy Against Bullying and Harassment

This policy was created with the support and guidance of the National Center for the Prevention of Community Violence. through a collaborative process with the community to include all interested stakeholders, school administrators, staff, students, families, and the greater community, in order to best address conditions in accordance with the student code of conduct.

It's purpose is to serve as a guideline for each school division to commit to a safe and civil educational environment for all students, employees, parents/legal guardians, volunteers, and patrons that are free from harassment, intimidation, or bullying.

The Model Policy, which follows, provides a framework for developing local plans. School divisions vary across the nation, but the fundamental approach is very thorough.

## Bullying Defined

Bullying can be described as systematically and chronically inflicting physical hurt or psychological distress on or by one or more students or employees.

It is further defined as unwanted and repeated written, verbal, or physical behavior, including any threatening, insulting, or dehumanizing gesture, by a student or adult, that is severe or pervasive enough to create an intimidating, hostile, or offensive educational environment; cause discomfort or humiliation; or unreasonably interfere with the individual's school performance or participation; and may involve but is not limited to:

- Teasing
- Social exclusion
- Threat
- Intimidation
- Stalking
- Physical Contact-(age and development of child considered)
- Theft
- Sexual, religious, or racial harassment
- Public humiliation
- Destruction of property

Bullying includes conduct that "substantially interferes with a student's education" and may be determined by considering a targeted student's grades, attendance, demeanor, interaction with peers, participation in activities, and other indicators.

Conduct that may rise to the level of harassment, intimidation, and bullying may take many forms, including, but not limited to; slurs, rumors, jokes, innuendoes, demeaning comments, drawings, cartoons, pranks, ostracism, physical attacks or threats, gestures, or acts relating to an individual or group whether electronic, written, oral, or physically transmitted messages or images.

There is no requirement that the targeted student actually possess the characteristic that is the basis for the harassment, intimidation, or bullying.

Cyberbullying/Cyber Stalking refers to any threats by one student toward another typically through e-mails or on web sites (e.g., blogs, social networking sites). Cyber stalking refers to a number of methods individuals use to track, lure, or harass another person online.

Bullying and Harassment also encompasses:

Bullying is also any act of retaliation against a student or school employee by another student or school employee for asserting or alleging an act of bullying or harassment. Reporting an act of bullying or harassment that is not made in good faith is considered retaliation.

In addition, the definition of bullying includes perpetuation of conduct listed in the definition of bullying or harassment by an individual or group with intent to demean, dehumanize, embarrass, or cause emotional or physical harm to a student or school employee by:

- Incitement or coercion
- Accessing or knowingly and willingly causing or providing access to data or computer software through a computer, computer system, or computer network within the scope of the school division's system
- Acting in a manner that has an effect substantially similar to the effect of bullying or harassment

The school district upholds that bullying or harassment of or by any student or school employee is prohibited:

- During any education program or activity conducted by a public K-12 educational institution
- During any school-related or school-sponsored program or activity
- On a school bus of a public K-12 educational institution
- During any community setting where the direct behavior or interaction of students would be carried over and have a negative impact on the academic setting of any public K-12 educational institution
- Through a communication device, computer system, or computer network in a K-12 education institution or off campus, which threatens a student or impairs his or her capacity to learn in school

## Related Definitions

**Aggressor/Bully**— is a student, staff member/employees, or other member of the school community who engages in the harassment, intimidation, or bullying of a student.

**Bystanders** — are persons who either instigate action or fail to respond to prevent or stop bullying behaviors. The bystander actions may include prodding the bully to initiate the behaviors or by laughing, cheering, or making comments that further encourage the bullying activity to continue or by remaining passive.

**Retaliation** — is defined as when an aggressor harasses, intimidates, or bullies a student who has reported incidents of bullying.

**Staff** — is defined to include, but is not limited to; educators, administrators, counselors, school nurses, cafeteria workers, custodians, bus drivers, athletic coaches, advisors to extracurricular activities, classified staff, substitute and temporary teachers, volunteers, or paraprofessionals (both employees and contractors).

**Targeted Student Victim** — is the student or students against whom harassment, intimidation, or bullying has allegedly been perpetrated.

## Prevention Strategies

The school division will implement a range of prevention strategies including individual, classroom, school, and district-level approaches.

## Compliance/Discipline Officer

The superintendent will appoint a compliance/discipline officer as the primary school division contact to receive copies of all formal and informal complaints and ensure policy implementation. The name and contact information for the compliance/discipline officer will be communicated throughout the school division in a means that is most accessible to students, parents, and staff.

The school division compliance/discipline officer will:

- Serve as the school division's primary contact for harassment, intimidation, and bullying
- Provide support and assistance to the principal or designee in resolving complaints
- Receive copies of all Incident Reporting Forms, discipline Referral Forms, and letters to parents providing the outcomes of investigations.
- Be familiar with the use of the student information system. The compliance officer may use this information to identify patterns of behavior and areas of concern
- Ensure implementation of the policy and procedure by overseeing the investigative processes, including ensuring that investigations are prompt, impartial, and thorough
- Assess the training needs of staff and students to ensure successful implementation throughout the school division, and ensure staff receive annual fall training

- Develop a procedure for maintaining written records of all incidents of bullying and their resolutions

## Dissemination

The school division and individual schools will prominently post information on reporting harassment, intimidation, and bullying on their Web sites. It will include the name and contact information for the school division compliance/discipline officer, and the name and contact information for making a report to a school administrator.

The school division's policy and procedure will be available in each school in a language that families can understand. Annually, the superintendent will ensure that a statement summarizing the policy and procedures is provided to students, staff and the community.

## Education

Annually students will receive age-appropriate information on the recognition and prevention of harassment, intimidation, or bullying at student orientation sessions and on other appropriate occasions. The information will include a copy of the Incident Reporting Form or a link to a Web-based form. Training

Staff will receive annual training on the school division's policy and procedure, including staff roles and responsibilities on how to identify bullying related behaviors and appropriate responses for immediate actions to address it.

## Investigating and Responding to Bullying

Includes a procedure for promptly investigating and responding to reports or incidents of bullying and protecting the victim from additional bullying or retaliation. This procedure will include notification to the parents of the victim of bullying, the parents of the alleged perpetrator, and if appropriate, notification to law enforcement officials.

## Step 1, Filing an Incident Report

Any student who believes he or she has been the target of unresolved, severe, or persistent harassment, intimidation, or bullying, or any other person in the school community who observes or receives notice that a student has or may have been the target of unresolved, severe, or persistent harassment, intimidation, or bullying, may report incidents verbally or in writing to any staff member.

In order to protect a targeted student from retaliation, he or she need not reveal his/her identity on an Incident Reporting Form. The form may be filed anonymously, confidentially, or the student may choose to disclose his or her identity (non-confidential). Schools should provide a copy of an Incident Reporting Form and/or make it available online.

### Status of Reporter

**Anonymous**—Individuals may file a report without revealing their identity. No disciplinary action will be taken against an alleged aggressor based solely on an anonymous report. Schools may identify complaint boxes or develop other methods for receiving anonymous, unsigned reports. Possible responses to an anonymous report include enhanced monitoring of specific locations at certain times of day or increased monitoring of specific students or staff. (Example: An unsigned Incident Reporting Form dropped on a teacher's desk led to the increased monitoring of the boys' locker room in 5th period.)

**Confidential**—Individuals may ask that their identities be kept secret from the accused and other students. Like anonymous reports, no disciplinary action will be taken against an alleged aggressor based solely on a confidential report. (Example: A student tells a playground supervisor about a classmate being bullied but asks that nobody know who reported the incident. The supervisor says, "I won't be able to punish the bullies unless you or someone else who saw it is willing to let me use their names, but I can start hanging out near the basketball court, if that would help.")

**Non-confidential**—Individuals may agree to file a report non-confidentially. Complainants agreeing to make their complaint non-confidential will be informed that due process requirements may require that the school division release all of the information that it has regarding the complaint to any individuals involved in the incident, but that even then, information will still be restricted to those with a need to know, both during and after the investigation. The school division will, however, fully implement the anti-retaliation provision of this policy and procedure to protect witnesses.

## Step 2. Receiving an Incident Report Form

All staff is responsible for receiving oral and written reports. Whenever possible, staff that initially receive an oral or written report of possible bullying shall attempt to resolve the incident immediately. If the incident is resolved to the satisfaction of the parties involved, or if the incident does not meet the definition of harassment, intimidation, or bullying, no further action may be necessary under this procedure.

## Step 3. Investigating

Upon receipt of a report of bullying, harassment, or cyberbullying the school principal or designee shall promptly conduct an investigation. When investigating the incidents within this policy all of the surrounding facts, circumstances, severity, and age/developmental appropriateness should be considered.

At each school in the school division, the Procedures for Investigating Bullying and/or Harassment include:

- The principal or designee selects a designee(s), employed by the school and trained in investigative procedures, to initiate the investigation. The designee(s) may not be the accused perpetrator (harasser or bully) or victim.

- Documented interviews of the victim, alleged perpetrator, and witnesses are conducted privately, separately, and are confidential. Each individual (victim, alleged perpetrator, and witnesses) will be interviewed separately and at no time will the alleged perpetrator and victim be interviewed together.
- The investigator shall collect and evaluate the facts including, but not limited to:
  - ◊ Description of incident(s) including nature of the behavior; context in which the alleged incident(s) occurred, etc.
  - ◊ How often the conduct occurred
  - ◊ Whether there were past incidents or past continuing patterns of behavior
  - ◊ The relationship between the parties involved
  - ◊ The characteristics of parties involved (i.e., grade, age, etc.)
  - ◊ The identity and number of individuals who participated in bullying or harassing behavior
  - ◊ Where the alleged incident(s) occurred
  - ◊ Whether the conduct adversely affected the student's education or educational environment
  - ◊ Whether the alleged victim felt or perceived an imbalance of power as a result of the reported incident
  - ◊ The date, time, and method in which the parents/legal guardians of all parties involved were contacted
  - ◊ Whether a particular action or incident constitutes a violation of this policy requires a determination based on all the facts and surrounding circumstances and includes recommended remedial steps necessary to stop the bullying and/or harassing behavior
  - ◊ A written final report to the principal
- The trained designee(s) will provide a report on results of investigation with recommendations for the principal to make a

determination if an act of bullying or harassment falls within the scope of the school division.

- The principal or designee may determine that other steps must be taken before the investigation is complete.
- The investigation will be started within five school days from the date of the initial report and completed within fifteen school days. If more time is needed to complete an investigation, the school division will provide the parent/guardian and/or the student with weekly updates.
- Following the completion of the investigation and the submission to the compliance/discipline officer, the principal or designee shall respond to the parent/guardian of the complainant and the alleged aggressor stating:
  - ◊ The results of the investigation
  - ◊ Whether the allegations were found to be factual
  - ◊ Whether there was a violation of policy
  - ◊ The process for the complainant to file an appeal if the complainant disagrees with results

By this policy to the parent or legal guardian of all students involved on the same day an investigation of the incident(s) has been initiated. To include steps to ensure safety and compliance to those involved. Notification must be consistent with the student privacy rights under the applicable provisions of the Family Educational Rights and Privacy Act of 1974 (FERPA), (20 U.S.C. § 1232g; 34 CFR Part 99).

If the school principal or designee determines that bullying or retaliation has occurred, the school principal or designee will take appropriate disciplinary action, notify the parents or guardians of the perpetrator, notify the parents or legal guardians of the victim, and if the school principal or designee believes that the situation is placing the victim in a position of harm or danger they shall notify local law enforcement.

Additionally, if the Principal believes a law has been violated than consultation with law enforcement is advised.

All reports of unresolved, severe, or persistent harassment, intimidation, or bullying will be recorded on a school division Incident Reporting Form and submitted to the principal or designee, unless the designee is the subject of the complaint, and to the compliance/discipline officer.

## Notification

A procedure is to be established for providing immediate notification to the parents/legal guardians of a victim of substantiated bullying or harassment and the parents or legal guardians of the perpetrator of an act of bullying or harassment as well as, notification to appropriate law enforcement agencies where criminal charges may be pursued against the perpetrator:

The principal, or designee, shall promptly report via telephone, personal conference, and/or in writing, the occurrence of any incident of bullying or harassment as defined by this policy to the parent or legal guardian of all students involved on the same day an investigation of the incident(s) has been substantiated. Notification must be consistent with the student privacy rights under the applicable provisions of the Family Educational Rights and Privacy Act of 1974 (FERPA).

Once the investigation has been completed and it has been determined that criminal charges may be pursued against the perpetrator, all appropriate law enforcement agencies will be notified by telephone and/or in writing.

## Statement of Rights to Other Legal Recourse

This policy may not be interpreted to prevent a victim of harassment, intimidation or bullying or a victim of cyberbullying from seeking redress or other legal remedies under any other available law, whether civil or criminal.

## Relationship to Other Laws

The school division will ensure its compliance with all state laws regarding harassment, intimidation or bullying. Nothing in this procedure prevents a student, parent/guardian, school or school division from taking action to remediate harassment or discrimination based on a person's membership in a legally protected class under local, state, or federal law.

## Procedure to Refer Victims and Perpetrators of Bullying or Harassment for Counseling

A school division referral procedure will establish a protocol for intervening when bullying or harassment is suspected or when a bullying incident is reported. The procedure shall include a process by which the teacher or parent/legal guardian may request informal consultation with school staff (specialty staff, e.g., school counselor, school psychologist, student assistance specialist/team, etc.) to determine the severity of concern and appropriate steps to address the concern (the involved students' parents or legal guardian may be included).

The referral process to provide professional assistance or services that includes a process by which school personnel or parent/legal guardian may refer a student to the school intervention team (or equivalent school-based team with a problem-solving focus) for consideration of appropriate services. (Parent or legal guardian involvement is required at this point.)

If a formal discipline report or formal complaint is made, the principal or designee must refer the student(s) to the school intervention team for determination of counseling support and interventions. (Parent or legal guardian involvement is required at this point.)

- A school-based component to address intervention and assistance as determined appropriate by the intervention team that includes:
  - ◊ Counseling and support to address the needs of the victims of bullying or harassment

◊ Research-based counseling/interventions to address the behavior of the students who bully and harass others (e.g., empathy training, anger management)

Research-based counseling/interventions which includes assistance and support provided to parents/legal guardians, if deemed necessary or appropriate.

# Acknowledgements

*This NCPCV Model Policy on Bullying and Harassment consulted model policies from around the country to create a comprehensive plan to address bullying. Model policies from the state of Virginia, Florida, Washington, and Massachusetts were used along with references from the policy proposed by the United States Department of Education.*

# Endnotes

## Solutions for Saving Our Children from Today's Bully

**Foreword**

**Introduction**

**What Not To Do When Encountering Today's Bully**

Microsoft Safety and Security Center, http://www.microsoft.com/security/resources/research.aspx.

**Contents**

### Preface — "Just Tell Me What To Do…"

**The Culture of Bullying — What Is It Really About and Why Are So Many Young People Embracing It?**

http://diversityinc.com/diversity-management/the-culture-of-bullying-loss-of-civility-at-school-work-politics/.
PBS website, www.pbs.org, PBS Frontline, The Merchants of Cool.

**Bullying Defined**

**How Bullying Got Out of Control**

**Bullying — Gaining Power and Control**

**Over the Life of Another**

Wikipedia, Wikipedia.com, http://en.wikipedia.org/wiki/Lord_of_the_Flies.

**Let's Dispel the Myths About Bullying**

**Understand All Five Traditional Forms of Bullying**

**At What Age Does Bullying Become a Danger to Kids?**

Civic Commons Radio Program Bullies Be Gone, Cleveland, Ohio, Hosts Dan Moulthrop and Noelle Celeste with Dr. Lisa Damour, April 10, 2012, http://theciviccommons.com/radioshow/bullies-be-gone.

**Distinguishing Between Meanness and Bullying**

**What Bullying and Gangs Have in Common**

## JUST TELL ME WHAT TO DO....

A Compilation of Suggested Solutions to Bullying Situations Parents, Teachers, Coaches and Family Members Will Encounter

## PREPARING OUR CHILDREN FOR BULLYING ENCOUNTERS

**Leave Nothing Unsaid with Your Child:**

**Have Regular "Bully Talks"**

StopBullying.gov
http://www.stopbullying.gov/prevention/talking-about-it/index.html.

http://www.eduguide.org/library/viewarticle/2139.
Jon Siebels, Talk with Your Children and Teenagers about Bullying
the Guitarist of Eve 6, in his blog on the Huffington Post, "School Bullying: To End It, We Must Change Our Culture." http://www.huffingtonpost.com/jon-siebels.

**Making the Distinction Between**

**Self-Esteem and Selfish Esteem**

http://nyti.ms/qcJoJ1.

**The Potential Impact of Bullying**

**Ten Suggestions to Help Your Child Navigate Around the Bullies**

**The Bully. The Victim. The Bystander.**

**Why Bystanders Have the Power**

Toni Nagi, The Bully Movement: An Interview With Lee Hirsch
Posted: 04/ 9/2012 http://www.huffingtonpost.com/toni-nagy/lee-hirsch-interview_b_1409208.html.

**Rehearse for the Show: Use Role
Play to Practice Reactions to Bullying**

**Kids May Not Love Every Classmate,
But They Understand Politeness**

http://www.pbs.org/thisemotionallife/blogs/your-child-resilient.
Maureen Healy, Growing Happy Kids: How to Foster Inner Confidence, Success and Happiness, PHealth Communications Inc., 2012.

**Differences and Diversity Are Wonderful, But Avoid Social Isolation**

http://www.huffingtonpost.com/wayne-maines/bullying_b_1460901.html.

Suicide Prevention Resource Center, http://www.sprc.org/sites/sprc.org/files/library/Suicide_Bullying_Issue_Brief.pdf. This paper was written by Effie Malley, Marc Posner, and Lloyd Potter with editorial and reference assistance provided by Lori Bradshaw and additional staff of the National Suicide Prevention Resource Center (SPRC). Suicide Prevention Resource Center. (2008). Suicide risk and prevention for lesbian, gay, bisexual, and transgender youth. Newton, MA: Education Development Center, Inc. This publication is available for download: http://www.sprc.org/library/SPRC_LGBT_Youth.pdf.

**Personality Will Impact How Your Child Responds to a Bullying Situation**

ScienceDaily Science News from universities, journals, and other research organizations, http://bit.ly/qgIr95, Aug. 30, 2011.

The study appears in the journal Child Development.

**Brothers and Sisters Will Have Conflict, Constantly; Minimize the Chaos By Not Buying Into the Provoking Behaviors**

Dan Moulthrop and Noelle Celeste with Dr. Lisa Damour, Civic Commons Radio Program Bullies Be Gone, Cleveland, Ohio, April 10, 2012 http://theciviccommons.com/radioshow/bullies-be-gone.

**Carefully Observe Your Child's Friends**

## EARLY WARNINGS

**Be Skeptical of Teasing**

Nancy Darling, Ph.D., Thinking About Kids, October 26, 2010 http://www.psychologytoday.com/blog/thinking-about-kids/201010/teasing-and-bullying-boys-and-girls.

EduGuide, "Is this Teasing or Bullying?" http://www.eduguide.org/.

**Watch for Warning Signs of Today's Bully**

Market Watch, Magellan Health Services Inc., Beyond the Bully and the Bullied: Bullying Also Impacts the Mental Health of the "Bystanders," May 9, 2012, http://www.marketwatch.com/story/beyond-the-bully-and-the-bullied-bullying-also-impacts-the-mental-health-of-the-bystanders-2012-05-09.

http://www.stopbullying.gov/at-risk/factors/index.html#morelikely.

**Is Your Child Becoming a Bully?**

**Be Alert to These Indicators**

By Parents for Parents website and blog, www.byparents-forparents.com/parenting/signs-that-your-child-is-being-bullied-at-school.html.

Jackson Katz and Sut Jhally, Put the Blame Where it Belongs: On Men By First published in The Los Angeles Times June 25, 2000, Sunday Commentary, Pg. M5 http://www.jacksonkatz.com/pub_blame.html.

Jessie Klein, THE BULLY SOCIETY—School Shootings and the Crisis of Bullying in America's Schools, New York University Press,

http://www.nytimes.com/2012/04/29/books/review/the-bully-society-by-jessie-klein.html.

Katz, Jackson website, www.Jacksonkatz.com.

## YOUR REACTION TO BULLYING

**Important Do's and Don'ts**

http://www.stopbullying.gov/respond/support-kids-involved/index.html.

**It Is a Crime to Assault Another Person; It Is Also a Civil Case.**

**The Four Things You Should Never Do**

http://www.stopbullying.gov/respond/support-kids-involved/index.html.

**Kids Can Be Slow to Reveal Being Bullied: Signs to Watch for.**

http://legal-dictionary.thefreedictionary.com/assault

http://mydoctor.kaiserpermanente.org/ncal/mdo/presentation/conditions/condition_viewall_page.jsp?condition=Health_Topic_Bullying_-_Pediatrics.xml&showProvider=true.

**The Five Kinds of Bullying Today**

Tom Morgan, Ignorance is No Defense: A Teenager's Guide to Georgia Law,

Westchester Legal Press; Second edition (February 1, 2009).

http://legal-dictionary.thefreedictionary.com/assault.

http://mydoctor.kaiserpermanente.org/ncal/mdo/presentation/conditions/

condition_viewall_page.jsp?condition=Health_Topic_Bullying_-_Pediatrics.xml&showProvider=true.

**Be Alert for Signs of Self-Harm Risk in a Bullied Child**

My Doctor Online, The Permanente Medical Group,

http://mydoctor.kaiserpermanente.org/ncal/mdo/presentation/conditions/condition_viewall_page.jsp?condition=Health_Topic_Bullying_-_Pediatrics.xml&showProvider=true.

The Suicide Prevention Resource Center (SPRC) is a project in EDC's Health and Human Development Division 43 Foundry Avenue, Waltham, MA 02453-8313. 877-GET-SPRC (438-7772), info@sprc.org.

M.A. Newton and P. Rogers, Suicide Prevention Resource Center, (2011). Understanding risk and protective factors for suicide: A primer for preventing suicide. Newton, MA: Education Development Center, Inc.
The Role of School Health and Mental Health Providers
in Preventing Suicide, Signs that a Young Person May Be at Risk for Suicide
http://www.sprc.org/sites/sprc.org/files/SchoolHealthMentalHealth.pdf
Kaltiala-Heino, Marttunen Rimpela, Bullying. children and adolescents, who are bullied, as well as those who bully, are at increased risk of depression and suicidal ideation (1999).
Jackson Katz website, www.Jacksonkatz.com.
Jackson Katz and Sut Jhally, Put the Blame Where it Belongs: On Men By
First published in The Los Angeles Times June 25, 2000, Sunday Commentary, Pg. M5 http://www.jacksonkatz.com/pub_blame.html.
Jessie Klein, THE BULLY SOCIETY—School Shootings and the Crisis of Bullying in America's Schools, New York University Press, http://www.nytimes.com/2012/04/29/books/review/the-bully-society-by-jessie-klein.html.

## SOCIAL MEDIA THREATS

**New Digital Dangers That May Be Invisible to Parents**

Yvonne Wenger, The Baltimore Sun, April 22, 2012
http://www.baltimoresun.com/news/maryland/howard/bs-md-ho-cyber-reader-20120422,0,1664908.story.
http://www.definetheline.ca/en/Welcome_Page_35.
"What is Cyber Bullying and How Can I Protect My Daughter?"
http://www.eduguide.com.
Jason Magder, The Montreal Gazette, February 13, 2012, http://www.montrealgazette.com/news/Tracking+down+online+outlaws/6142983/story.html#ixzz1ss2t2fOK.

John Potter, WTVN Channel 2 News, Facebook Targets Online Bullies http://www.ktvn.com/story/19020452/facebook-targets-online-bullies.

**You Are Paying the Bill: Control Your Child's Social Media**

http://www.stopbullying.gov/respond/support-kids-involved/index.html.
Education.com, http://www.education.com.

**When Cyberbullying Becomes a Crime**

http://www.stopbullying.gov/respond/support-kids-involved/index.html.

## THE BULLYING CHILD

**Physical Bullying Is a Boys' World**

Jackson Katz website, www.Jacksonkatz.com.

Jackson Katz and Sut Jhally, Put the Blame Where it Belongs: On Men By First published in The Los Angeles Times June 25, 2000, Sunday Commentary, Pg. M5 http://www.jacksonkatz.com/pub_blame.html.

Jessie Klein, THE BULLY SOCIETY—School Shootings and the Crisis of Bullying in America's Schools, New York University Press,

http://www.nytimes.com/2012/04/29/books/review/the-bully-society-by-jessie-klein.html.

**Girl Bullies Use Different Weapons**

Cheryl Dellasega and Charisse Nixon, Girl Wars: 12 Strategies That Will End Female Bullying [Paperback] Fireside; Original edition (October 7, 2003).

Girls Who Bully: What, When, Where, Why, and How http://www.eduguide.org/library/viewarticle/2118/.

Patricia A. Farrell, PhD, and Susan Davis; WebMD the Magazine — Feature,
WebMD the Magazine — Feature,
http://www.webmd.com/parenting/features/mean-girls-why-girls-bully-and-how-to-stop-them.

**If Your Child Becomes a Bully, New Ground Rules Are Essential**

My Doctor Online, The Permanente Medical Group,
http://mydoctor.kaiserpermanente.org/ncal/mdo/presentation/conditions/.

## THE BULLIED CHILD

**Confronting the Parents**

**Teach Your Child to Stand Firm**

Highlights — Parents, http://www.highlightsparents.com/parenting_perspectives/three_experts_answer_your_questions_about_bullying.

**Twelve Things to Consider When Your Child Has Been Bullied**

http://www.stopbullying.gov/respond/support-kids-involved/index.html.

**Bullying of Any Kind Can Result in Lifelong Emotional Damage and Why Professional Counseling Should Be Considered**

http://www.education.com/reference/article/Ref_What_Happens_Over/?page=2.
Patricia McDougall, Shelley Hymel and Tracy Vaillancourt, PhD,
Bullying Special Edition Contributor, Education.com, What Happens Over Time To Those Who Bully And Those Who Are Victimized?
Market Watch, Magellan Health Services Inc., Beyond the Bully and the Bullied: Bullying Also Impacts the Mental Health of the "Bystanders," May 9, 2012, http://www.marketwatch.com/story/beyond-the-bully-

and-the-bullied-bullying-also-impacts-the-mental-health-of-the-bystanders-2012-05-09.

**Do Children Grow Out of Bullying?**

Patricia McDougall, Shelley Hymel and Tracy Vaillancourt, PhD
Bullying Special Edition Contributor, Education.com, What Happens Over Time To Those Who Bully And Those Who Are Victimized?
Suicide Prevention Resource Center, http://www.sprc.org/sites/sprc.org/files/library/Suicide_Bullying_Issue_Brief.pdf.
Psychology Today, http://therapists.psychologytoday.com/rms/name/Beth_Bennett-Hill_MDiv, LPC_Charlotte_North+Carolina_37204.
EMDR: The Breakthrough "Eye Movement" Therapy for Overcoming Anxiety, Stress, and Trauma by Francine Shapiro the discoverer and developer of this treatment.
http://www.emdr-therapy.com/emdr.html.

**Get Involved and Monitor Your Child's School Environment**

http://curry.virginia.edu/press-releases/study-students-fare-better-in-schools-that-dont-apply-automatic-expulsion.
Kotz, Deborah Globe Staff, Boston.com, Daily Dose, 'Bully' film highlights secrecy of bullying: 5 steps to combat it, April 12, 2012
http://www.boston.com/Boston/dailydose/2012/04/bully-film-highlights-secrecy-bullying-steps-combat/nv4mxbCvKqoONw3fsXcEmK/index.html.
http://www.stopbullying.gov/respond/support-kids-involved/index.html.
Curry School of Education, http://curry.virginia.edu/news/updates/nbc29-features-anti-bullying-survey-developed-by-youth-nex-researcher-corne.
Office of Juvenile Justice and Delinquency. Juvenile Justice Bulletin,
December 2011 edition, http://www.ojjdp.gov/pubs/234205.pdf.
StopBullying.gov
http://www.stopbullying.gov/prevention/talking-about-it/index.html.

# YOUTH SPORTS

**Adult Bully Behavior Needs to Be Challenged**

Sarah Harris, Mail Online, April 15, 2012, http://www.dailymail.co.uk/news/article-2130233/Victims-sport-bullies-aged-Pupils-tell-psychological-warfare-playing-field.html#ixzz1srxUD4JV.

# Bibliography

American Association of Suicidology, Prevention Division. (1999). Guidelines for school based suicide prevention programs. Washington, DC: American Association of Suicidology.

Cavell, T., and Smith, A.M. 2005. Mentoring children. In *Handbook of Youth Mentoring*, edited by D.L. DuBois and M.J. Karcher. Thousand Oaks, CA: Sage Publications, pp. 160–176.

Dellasega, Cheryl and Charisse Nixon, *Girl Wars: 12 Strategies That Will End Female Bullying*, Fireside; Original edition (October 7, 2003).

Elias, M. J. (2006). The connection between academic and social-emotional learning. In M. J. Elias & H. Arnold (Eds.), *The educator's guide to emotional intelligence and academic achievement: Social-emotional learning in the classroom* (pp. 4-14). Thousand Oaks, CA: Corwin Press.

Jimerson, S.R., Swearer, S.M., and Espelage, D.L., eds. 2010. *Handbook of Bullying in Schools*. New York, NY: Routledge.

Newton, M.A., Suicide Prevention Resource Center. (2008). Suicide risk and prevention for lesbian, gay, bisexual, and transgender youth. Education Development Center, Inc. Retrieved from http://www.sprc.org/library/SPRC_LGBT_Youth.pdf.

Olweus, D. (1993b). Victimisation by peers: Antecedents and long-term outcomes. In K.H. Rubin and J.B. Asendorpf (eds.) *Social withdrawal, inhibition and shyness in childhood* (pp. 315-341), Erlbaum, Hillsdale, NJ.

Olweus, D. (1993). *Bullying at School: What We Know and What We Can Do.* Williston, VT: Blackwell Publishers.

Olweus, D. (1997). "Bully/Victim Problems in School: Knowledge Base and an Effective Intervention Program," *The Irish Journal of Psychology,* 18, 170-190.

Olweus, D., Limber, S., & Mihalic, S. (1999). *Blueprints for violence prevention, book nine: bullying prevention program,* Boulder, CO: Center for the Study and Prevention of Violence.

Pickhardt, C. (2002). *Why Kids Act Cruel: The Hidden Truth about the Preteen Years.* Sourcebooks, Inc.

Rudd, M. D., Berman, A. L., Joiner, T. E., Jr., Nock, M. K., Silverman, M. M., Mandrusiak, M., et al. (2006). Warning signs for suicide: Theory, research, and clinical applications, *Suicide and Life-Threatening Behavior,* 36(3), 255-262.

Ryan, C., Russell, S. T., Huebner, D., Diaz, R., & Sanchez, J. (2010). Family acceptance in adolescence and the health of LGBT young adults, *Journal of Child and Adolescent Psychiatric Nursing,* 23(4), 205-213.

Salmivalli, C. (2001). Group view on victimization: Empirical findings and their implications. J. Juvonen & S. Graham (Eds.). *Peer harassment in school: The plight of the vulnerable and the victimized,* (pp. 398-419). New York: The Guilford Press.

Simmons, R. (2002). *Odd Girl Out: The Hidden Culture of Aggression in Girls.* Orlando, FL: Harcourt.

Suicide Prevention Resource Center, & Rodgers, P. (2011). *Understanding risk and protective factors for suicide: A primer for preventing suicide.* Newton, MA: Education Development Center, Inc.

Swearer, Susan M., Espelage, Dorothy L., and Napolitano, Scott A., *Bullying Prevention and Intervention: Realistic Strategies for Schools,* The Guilford Practical Intervention in the Schools Series), The Guilford Press; 1 edition (January 21, 2009).

Ttofi, M.M., Farrington, D.P., and Baldry, A.C. 2008.

*Effectiveness of Programmes to Reduce School Bullying: A Systematic Review*, Stockholm, Sweden: Swedish National Council for Crime Prevention.

U.S. Department of Health and Human Services (2001). *National Strategy for Suicide Prevention: Goals and Objectives for Action*, Rockville, MD: Author, Public Health Service. (See http://store.samhsa.gov/product/SMA01-3517).

U.S. Centers for Disease Control and Prevention. (n.d.). Promoting Individual, Family, and Community Connectedness to Prevent Suicidal Behavior. Retrieved from http://www.cdc.gov/violenceprevention/pdf/suicide_strategic_direction_full_version-a.pdf.

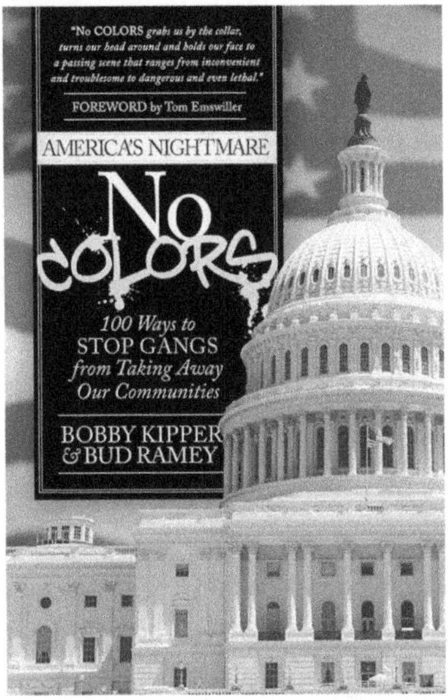


*Available on Amazon.com, Barnes & Noble and www.solveviolence.com*

***"No COLORS"***
released by
Morgan James Publishing,
New York

New York, NY — "***No COLORS: 100 Ways to Stop Gangs from Taking Away Our Communities***" (Morgan James Publishing, February 2012, $19.95, Paperback), one of the most relevant nonfiction books of the year, responds to the youth violence crisis now threatening the fabric of America. Through significant research and first-hand experiences, authors Bobby Kipper and Bud Ramey are able to present community solutions that are proven to work.

The FBI's October 2011 National Gang Threat Assessment reports a shocking 40% increase in U.S. gang membership in just the last two years. With over 1.4 million gang members in America, the report shows that gangs are no longer confined to urban areas. "It's here now. It's lethal. It's an epidemic. Gangs are spreading to the quiet suburbs, gated communities, small towns…" Ramey and Kipper note.

"***No COLORS***" is a warning.

"This is much more than a melancholy episode in the growth of communities. It's all on the line here for your hometown and police cannot handle it alone."

***"No COLORS"*** is ultimately a story of hope.

Community leaders, parents, business leaders, civic groups, the faith community find here a guide to what is working across the U.S. and abroad. Kipper and Ramey provide optimism to a situation that seemingly grows more hopeless daily.

They dispel common myths — that members can never leave a gang, that all kids in gangs are violent offenders, and that only police can solve the problem. It is essential to reconnect high-risk youth to their schools, families, communities and ultimately, their futures. The authors want readers to understand that "We can't win this with arrests."

Bobby Kipper is founder of the National Center for the Prevention of Community Violence. A battle-hardened ex-cop with a quarter century of community policing in one of America's toughest gang environments, Kipper organized one of the most effective crime prevention programs ever developed by the Justice Department. He has consulted for the White House, Congress, and governors and for communities across America.

Bud Ramey is the 2010 Public Affairs Silver Anvil Award winner of the Public Relations Society of America—the highest public affairs recognition in the world. His grassroots public affairs and humanitarian successes stretch across three decades.

**www.solveviolence.com**

National Center for the Prevention of Community Violence

**www.solveviolence.com**

"We are passionate about prevention, intervention, enforcement and re-entry strategies. We are passionate about measurement and even more passionate about saving our children from bullying, gangs and community violence."

**NCPCV Mission**

Our Mission is to create new pathways for communities to react with passion to the wave of youth violence sweeping America and Canada, and to share what we have learned with every community we can engage in the crisis.

**"THERE IS SOMETHING WE CAN DO ABOUT THE EPIDEMIC OF YOUTH VIOLENCE"**

**NCPCV Accomplishments**

- Creator of "***No COLORS: 100 Ways to Stop Gangs from Taking Away our Communities***
- Creator of "***No BULLIES, Solutions for Saving Our Children from Today's Bully***"
- Partnering with Virginia Tech's Center for Applied Behavioral Sciences. This joint partnership will work in developing new practice models to combat bullying, gangs, and youth violence
- Developed model bullying policy for the Virginia Department of Education
- Developed and implemented a Gun Safety Program for the Commonwealth of Virginia Board of Education for students K-5
- Developing Athlete-Coach mentoring for anti-gang programs at Old Dominion University Athletic Department
- Training and educating police officers in working with troubled youth in Memphis, TN, Newport News and other communities
- Co-sponsoring series of Annual Bullying Conferences for educators with Children's Hospital of The King's Daughters (CHKD) and Christopher Newport University
- Directed America's top crime prevention efforts in Richmond, Virginia: Gang Reduction and Intervention Program (G.R.I.P)
- Creator of *The Green Zone*, anti-bullying and civility campaign program.

We welcome your inquiries regarding helping your community reduce youth violence and gangs. Send us an email at and let us know how we can help to rjkandassociates@cox.net.

**Who We Are**

The National Center for the Prevention of Community Violence, located in Eastern Virginia, is a nonprofit 501c(3) organization that conducts research, training, and evaluation on violence prevention efforts around the United States. This organization offers project management and evaluation services with a goal of directing best practice resources toward tangible results.

Our affiliates and volunteers have been honored with the top award in the nation for crime prevention (International Association of Chiefs of Police 2008) and top international award for public affairs (Public Relations Society of America, Silver Anvil for Public Affairs 2010). We are committed to helping communities make good decisions in responding to the crisis of gangs and youth violence, available to you to help create positive change by shaping your resources to build sustained capacity for success.

A big part of our Mission is to help communities establish a Strategic Plan, and provide appropriate resources to deal with this crisis. And then spread the news about what measurable tactics that are working.

The Chairman of the Board of NCPCV is David Hancock, founder and CEO of Morgan James Publishing, one of the most prominent and sought-after publishers in the nation.

**Board of Directors | NCPCV**

***Bobby Kipper***

Director, National Center for the Prevention of Community Violence

***David Hancock***

Founder and CEO of Morgan James Publishing

***Bud Ramey***

2010 Public Relations Society of America Public Affairs Silver Anvil Award Winner

**National Center for the Prevention of Community Violence**

4410 East Claiborne Square, Suite 334 | Hampton, VA 23666

6580 Gardenoak Court, San Jose, CA 95120

Telephone: 757-251-3767 | Fax:757-251-3801

Email: rjkandassociates@cox.net

# GREEN ZONE

| Behavior | Recommended Intervention |
| --- | --- |
| Using a normal rate, tone, and volume of speech | (None) |
| Complimenting or encouraging others | (None) |
| Informally questioning others | (None) |
| Joking in a non-harmful manner | (None) |

# YELLOW ZONE

| Behavior | Recommended Intervention |
| --- | --- |
| Name-calling and put-downs | Group intervention *and* individual intervention as necessary |
| Intentionally excluding individuals | Group intervention *and* individual intervention as necessary. |
| Damaging another's reputation | Group intervention *and* individual intervention as necessary. |
| Spreading rumors | Group intervention *and* individual intervention as necessary. |
| Manipulating friendships or other relationships | Group intervention *and* individual intervention as necessary. |

# RED ZONE

| Behavior | Recommended Intervention |
| --- | --- |
| Using profane or abusive language | Individual intervention and legal consequences if necessary. |
| Threatening or intimidating others | Individual intervention and legal consequences if necessary. |
| Harassing others based on their race, gender, sexual orientation, personal beliefs, or any other physical or personal characteristic. | |

# The *Green Zone*™

**Introducing the *GreenZone*,** a powerful new, measurable, and affordable anti-bullying and civility campaign for schools and public venues.

**"Imagine living in a world where everyone treated each other with respect; a world without insults, profanity, or threats, where everyone spoke to each other using a normal rate, tone and volume of speech. If this is the environment you wish to live and be involved with, welcome to the *GreenZone*™.**

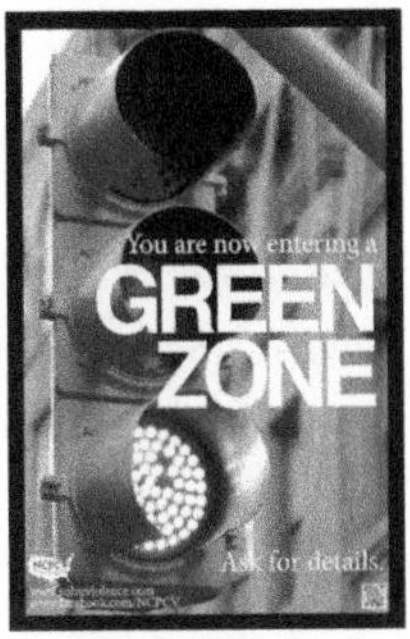


*The GreenZone* is a road to civility encouraging positive social interaction and appropriate conversation. The *GreenZone* concept introduces individuals to a color-coded outline of civil and uncivil behavior. Everyone who enters a setting designated as a *GreenZone* agrees to exhibit the respectful behaviors outlined in the *Green Zone.* If this zone is left, individuals will be called to accountability.

Encouraging individuals to stay in the green zone will create a safe, civil, and comfortable environment for all those who are in it.

**Goals**

- To introduce prevention and intervention models to cultivate respectful, productive civil behavior, and transform disrespectful, destructive behavior.
- To establish *GreenZone*™ schools/classrooms, community centers, social organizations, public centers, homes, and businesses throughout communities.
- To model, restore, foster and sustain civility in communities across the globe.

**For more information on the *GreenZone*™, visit our website at www.solveviolence.com.**

# ACTIVELY CARING FOR PEOPLE

On April 16th, 2007, a shooter, bullied since elementary school, killed 32 people and injured several others on the Virginia Tech campus in Blacksburg, Virginia. As a response, Dr. E. Scott Geller and his students at Virginia Tech initiated a culture shift on campus—the Actively Caring for People movement. This large-scale initiative aims to establish a more compassionate, interdependent, and empathic culture within schools, businesses, organizations, and throughout entire communities.

## HOW IT WORKS

The phrase "actively caring," coined by Dr. Geller, Alumni Distinguished Professor and leader of Virginia Tech's Center for Applied Behavior Science, refers to "any behavior going above and beyond the call of duty on behalf of the health, welfare, or well-being of another person." The Actively Caring for People (AC4P) movement encourages individuals to exhibit actively caring behavior, or to perform intentional acts of kindness as part of their daily routine. The positive exchanges between individuals, resulting from actively-caring behaviors *and* its supportive recognition, has a mutually reinforcing effect, leading to an actively-caring culture.

Following the launch of AC4P, thousands of green, actively-caring wristbands were distributed across the country to individuals performing acts of caring with the instructions to pay it forward, by passing on the wristband, when he or she observes someone else performing an act of kindness. By using the wristband to recognize actively-caring behavior, a tangible reminder of kindness is associated with the feeling of self- transcendence.

Today, there are thousands of actively-caring wristbands circulating the entire globe. Each wristband is engraved with a number that recipients may enter into the AC4P online database. Doing so helps to identify how far the wristbands have traveled, and helps to foster an online community of caring.

# Actively Caring for People, A Character-Education Approach to Bullying Prevention

In the Summer of 2009, Dr. E. Scott Geller, Shane McCarty and Taris Mullins developed an intervention program to reduce bullying behavior, increase compassion, and increase belonging in elementary schools. In the Fall of 2009, a single Fairfax, VA school assisted with survey development and program enhancement ideas to pilot the program. Since this pilot, schools from across the United States have implemented the program with outstanding success.

## How It Works

At the elementary school level, AC4P helps transform schools into positive environments full of actively caring individuals. The AC4P system designed for elementary school students is simple: students see others doing acts of kindness, write caring stories of their observations, and receive recognition with a green wristband.

More specifically, students look for actively-caring behavior (i.e. any behavior that goes beyond the call of duty to help others) in the classroom and write caring stories on a note card if they see a classmate doing something kind or sharing. Instructors then read a few caring stories at the beginning of each day and choose the kind student *and* observer of the kind act to wear the actively-caring wristbands for the day. After every student in the classroom has worn the wristband once, everyone in the class will get a band to wear permanently.

To learn more about Actively Caring for People, visit www.ac4p.org.

# AC4P & Green Zone™, Revolutionary Processes

The missions of Actively Caring for People and Green Zone™ are strikingly similar. For this reason, Dr. E. Scott Geller and Bobby Kipper, Director of The National Center for the Prevention of Community Violence, have joined hands to help promote kindness and civility in an effort to make both schools and communities safer places for individuals of all ages.

## Why Revolutionary?

Until now, the majority of well-respected and widely implemented initiatives to discourage acts of violence have approached the issue beginning with the end result. In other words, "solutions" to violence—and bullying in particular—have largely been approached from a responsive, disciplinary standpoint. This model of approach focuses on *consequences*, addressing issues *after* they occur.

AC4P and Green Zone™ are revolutionary processes in that they focus on overall environment rather than individual action. In doing so, they address problematic issues *before* they occur. Rather than focusing on discipline and trying to reach solutions "after the fact," Green Zone™ and AC4P focus on *transforming culture*. This focus on culture, not consequence, is both revolutionary and incredibly important for fostering safe and civil environments in schools and communities alike.

This revolutionary and broadened focus on the issue of violence prevention is reason for AC4P and Green Zone™ to be deemed *processes*, not *programs* in their essence. *Programs* tend to have a beginning and end, and often promise a desired end result. For both Green Zone™ and AC4P, the goal is not 0% violence or 0% bullying in a single school, but rather a culture shift—a change in mindset and thus a change in culture, a culture that encourages kind acts instead of violence and promotes positivity and civility overall. AC4P and

Green Zone™are processes that mark the cornerstone in a movement that will help shift culture from the present norm to the norm we all hope for.

1 www.ac4p.org
2 www.ac4p.org
3 www.ac4p.org
4 i.e., the Olweus Bullying Prevention Program

Printed in the USA
CPSIA information can be obtained
at www.ICGtesting.com
JSHW022137060524
62644JS00005B/472

9 781614 484370